POCKET MAN
The Unauthorized Autobiography of a Passionate, Personal Promoter

By Scott Jordan
with Thom O'Leary

Elevator Pitch: This Book in a Nutshell

Since starting SCOTTeVEST in 2000 - my clothing business built around tech-enabled pockets - I've been featured in thousands of major press pieces, made millions of dollars and had the most memorable appearance of the entire ABC *Shark Tank* show.

I started out as an unhappy lawyer, and I reinvented myself by pursuing my passions and mastering the art of passionate, personal promotion.

This isn't a how to business book, but entrepreneurs will learn a lot from my successes and failures about how to get the attention every business needs to stand above the competition.

This isn't fiction, but some of the stories might make you wonder if they are true. I assure you... they are.

Imagine Bill Gates and Giorgio Armani started a business, then hired PT Barnum to promote it, and Larry David to tell the story. The result is this book.

We're going to turn the world of media upside down, shake it and see what falls out of its pockets. You will learn lots of ways to promote yourself and your business, if you have the fire.

Welcome to my unauthorized autobiography. Why "unauthorized?" My lawyers suggested it because of what's in Chapter 4 (don't skip ahead... the payoff is worth the journey getting there).

Why Should You Listen to Me?

1. The clothing company I founded and still run to this day - SCOTTeVEST - was the first clothing brand launched on the internet that still exists.

2. SCOTTeVEST has made over $50 million to date.

3. My company has been self-funded from day one, and (highly) profitable from year one.

4. We have been featured in the *INC. Magazine* Fastest Growing companies list for several years and won numerous *Internet Retailer* Hot 100 awards.

5. I appeared on the highest rated episode of ABC's *Shark Tank* (up to that point), and have been shown in most of their major promos ever since. If you haven't seen it... I told the Sharks they were out, then walked out.

6. My customers include: Steve Wozniak, Matthew McConaughey, Dustin Hoffman, LeVar Burton, Adam Baldwin, Michael Mann, Adam West, Joe Mantegna, Wayne Brady, Rachael Ray, Herbie Hancock, Andrew McCarthy, Brad Thor, Andrew Zimmern, Jeff Bezos, Dave Barry, Scott Turow and dozens of other celebrities and influencers. (See www.scottevest.com/celebs)

7. I have created a pocket empire by selling clothing containing over 10 million pockets to customers in 188 countries.

8. I am responsible for securing *thousands* of media placements and articles in outlets like the *New York Times*, *Wall Street Journal*, *TIME Magazine*, *The Today Show*, ABC, NBC, CBS and CNN... without a PR firm. There are over 258K references to SCOTTeVEST on Google.

9. SCOTTeVEST has been in feature films like *Sahara* (worn by Matthew McConaughey), in 10 episodes of NBC's *CHUCK*, ABC's *Flash Forward*, the *Today Show* and *Good Morning*

America. I was even the subject of a Japanese TV show titled *The World's Most Successful People.* (Yeah, that one was a little weird.)

10. There have been over 7 million unique visitors and 60 million page views on the SCOTTeVEST site. We now average over 1 million page views per month, and my company and I have nearly 100K social media followers.

11. I have been the subject of full page profiles in *Entrepreneur* and *Fast Company* magazines, and have been featured on the TV show *The Big Idea with Donny Deutsch.*

12. SCOTTeVEST has worked with Intel, Google and the FBI. The FBI even awarded me a plaque based on the importance of SCOTTeVEST to fulfilling their (secret) missions.

13. My patented TEC-Technology Enabled Clothing® system has been licensed by The North Face, Nautica, Polo Ralph Lauren, Calvin Klein, Under Armour and many other major brands.

14. Steve Wozniak, co-founder of Apple, and Hap Klopp, founder of The North Face are on the SCOTTeVEST board.

15. Don't believe me? *Fortune* magazine said, "Imagine Giorgio Armani and Bill Gates stranded on a desert island and you'll have a good idea of what [SCOTTeVEST] has to offer."

16. I have been able to support charities that matter to me in a major way.

17. Every day, I get to do what I want, when I want... and I did most of it from a sleepy mountain town (aka paradise) in Idaho.

I accomplished all this because I mastered the art of passionate, personal promotion, and this book will show you exactly how I did it. I am clearly living my version of the American Dream... and I firmly believe you can too.

Foreword
by Steve Wozniak

I've known Scott Jordan for awhile. I first came to know him because he created an interesting product - the SCOTTeVEST - and I love interesting products that make our lives better.

I know him because he's an interesting person. Go ahead and ask him... he'll tell you he's interesting, too!

I first discovered SCOTTeVEST because whenever I travel, I need to wear clothes... mostly because of airline regulations, but also because I was not born with enough pockets to carry all my gadgets with me. Scott's clothing is the best for travel because it has dozens of hidden pockets and I can carry all the geeky gadgets and toys that make life convenient and fun.

When Scott first told me he was writing a book called "Pocket Man," I thought it sounded like a superhero story. In a way, it is. Everyone who starts out with a vision and a dream to make the world better in some small way or some large way can be a superhero. Doing the work to make that vision a reality can be hard, but it's necessary, and Scott has done it.

Scott adds fun and usefulness to the world with his visionary products, and now with his excellent book. One parting thought: whatever you do, don't imagine William Shatner performing "Pocket Man" in the style of "Rocket Man." I guarantee it'll be in your head the whole time you read the book.

Ask Scott... a little mischief can be fun, right? That's what makes interesting people like Scott... interesting.

- ʞɐıuzoM ǝʌǝʇs

6

Blurbs

"If there's anything I appreciate, it's good hockey. And evangelism. This book explains how to rock as an evangelist... which is good because Scott can't skate to save his life." **Guy Kawasaki**, chief evangelist of Canva and former chief evangelist of Apple

"Not only is Scott's book entertaining, but it has a nice sound when you hit it. What other book is also a great, pocket-sized percussion instrument? Bravo!" – **Herbie Hancock**, Grammy-winning Jazz Legend

"Scott who? The vest guy? Yeah, his book rocks. Wait, this is his book? Oh, cool." – **Robert Scoble**, Rackspace Startup Liaison Officer

"As an expert on army ants and jungles, I can tell you this book is infested. With a wild, adventurous spirit, I mean." – **Mark Moffett**, National Geographic's "Indiana Jones of Entomology"

"I've been an evangelist of what Scott has built, and yes, even of Scott, since I first discovered his first vest in 2001. I've tried to help him over the years when it involved PR and Marketing. He always took my advice, then did whatever the hell he wanted anyway." - **Peter Shankman**, Marketing and PR All-Star

"Scott Jordan took tech clothing and made it chic while pocketing millions and now he's showing you how to sew your own empire!" - **Jeffrey Hayzlett**, Primetime TV Show Host, Bestselling Author & Sometime Cowboy

"I've read so many first time authors book previews and they all have one thing in common, they suck... Much to my surprise, it was really good. I don't mean just ok, or passable, or good for a first timer. But really friggin good. If you want to know the art of self-promotion and stop wasting time and money with flaky PR firms, then read this book." – **Rick Wilson**, President of Miva Merchant

"A highly entertaining and enjoyable book that dissects the brilliance of SCOTTeVEST while simultaneously teaching things they never teach you in business school, but should." – **Hap Klopp**, Founder and former CEO of The North Face and author of *Conquering The North Face*

Dedication

The idea for this book originated years ago as a self-promotion tactic. Honestly, I wanted to go on a book tour without having to write a book. But through the process of a half-dozen false starts, I discovered something entirely unexpected: there was a book inside of me that actually needed to see the light of day.

Writing this book was an interesting process, but my wife Laura was there when I lived it. You'll read about me on my darkest days at the bottom of a ditch and when I was standing on top of a mountain, both literally and figuratively, and she stood behind me in every situation. (Usually, she stood behind me so she'd have more leverage to push....)

Without her, there would be no Scott, no SCOTTeVEST, no book and no joy from raising our family of poodles: Chloe, Margaux and Susie, or their sisters Lucy and Kelly who are already in another life. It seems like everything that is good about me is due to the women in my life: my mom, my poodles and especially Laura.

So this book is dedicated to Laura, who put her whole confidence in me while I made my dreams reality. She is a co-founder in our business and she is a driving force behind every story I tell, even though she'd rather stay in the background most of the time. This book is dedicated to my wife who told me sincerely that I could do whatever I wanted to do in life, even if that meant leaving behind my prosperous law career to dedicate myself to becoming a world-famous yoga instructor.

It was a stretch - pun intended - but she meant it.

I had never received that level of support from anyone in my life, and it means more to me than she could ever know. She works tirelessly for SCOTTeVEST and the Scott behind it (that's me) for 12 hours a day to make sure every order gets processed, and the world of pockets keeps turning.

Laura is the foundation of everything that means anything in my life, and that is why this book is dedicated to her.

Scott Jordan
Pocket Man, CEO & Founder, SCOTTeVEST

Introduction

A lot of CEOs, inventors and business people write a book at some point in their career when they feel like "the world" needs to hear their opinions on things.

They usually start with some sort of early childhood stories about how they did a lemonade stand in their parents' driveway, or had a paper route, or started a dog-walking business. They made more money in their first two weeks than you ever made before, and they caught the entrepreneurial bug! Yay for them!

This is NOT that kind of book.

Yes, I am a CEO. Yes, I am incredibly successful, and in fact many people would even say I am successful in spite of myself.

It has nothing to do with my paper route as a kid, though I did have one. It has nothing to do with "catching the entrepreneurial bug," but I do have it. It has nothing to do with having the best customer service, the best employees, the best product or the best commitment to quality, but my company and I have all those things.

It boils down this:

I AM A SHAMELESS, PASSIONATE, PERSONAL PROMOTER.

If you are a business owner or entrepreneur whose business isn't doing so well, sorry, but you're doing something wrong.

If you don't have the passion to promote yourself, you need to re-evaluate your choice of career.

The good news is that if YOU are doing something wrong, you can fix it. I did a lot of things wrong, but the things I did right, I did really, really right.

This book is a call to all would-be entrepreneurs, current business owners, people who are stuck in their 9-to-5 jobs and anyone who feels like they're not getting everything out of life they could... you need to promote yourself.

It's not very hard, but it requires putting yourself on the line. It's not expensive. It's not terribly time-consuming. But it does require you to change your thinking on one vital topic: you need to get fired up by rejection more than you are discouraged by it.

This is how I did it, and you can too. I'm not going to tell you how to get millions of dollars in free mass media exposure (including national TV), but I'm going to tell you how I did it. I'm not going to pontificate about how my way is the only way, but it's the only way I know has worked for me with 100% certainty. I'm not a guru, but if you pay attention, you'll learn something.

What This Book Is About

There are going to be parts of this book you're not going to like.

Wait... what?

I said, "There are going to be parts of this book you're not going to like."

Ok, so ask yourself this: what kind of author starts out a book with a statement like that? The answer is simple in this case: an author who is unapologetically committed to transparency, can't help but speak his mind, and wants this reading experience to be unlike anything you've ever seen before.

I'm in the driver's seat, and we're going to go on a ride that explores how I was able to bring my company SCOTTeVEST from an idea created by a desperately unhappy man into being the vehicle for my happiness and personal freedom.

If you keep reading I will guarantee that you will not be bored, and you may even learn a thing or twenty about how I've been able to make my clothing business (the first clothing brand started completely online) incredibly successful despite lawyers, liars, flakes, terrorists, Sharks, shitty technology, focus groups, PR agents, compromisers and even my own worst enemy... myself.

Bottom Line:

80% of this book is about how to use exploit/leverage media* to promote yourself and your business, but it's up to you to read between the lines and see how to apply it to your situation.

* In my book – which is this book – "media" consists of everything that comes out of your mouth, pen, typewriter, iPhone, Siri and video camera. The goal is the get it to the largest audience possible.

Some Background: What My Company Is About

When I started SCOTTeVEST, pockets in clothing hadn't been given any special thought since Levi Strauss added the fifth pocket on his jeans to hold the most popular gadget of his day. Since that was around the turn of the last century, his pocket innovation was designed to hold - drumroll, please - a pocket watch.

But what I found even more inspirational was that by adding a rivet to reinforce the strain points on his pants, he created a functional improvement and a brand statement in one step. He took something that is pretty obvious and with his business partner developed a patent around it.

I applied the same types of thinking to my creation. I started by considering what people carry, and I built pockets around those items (but to a much more extreme degree). If his pocket innovation was a bicycle, mine would be a flying car.

I also took a very obvious idea – like his rivet – and created a functional, useful, patented innovation. My invention allows wires to be run between pockets through the lining of a piece of clothing, which is essential for recharging devices and keeping headphones untangled. Simple, but pretty revolutionary, too.

I built my pocket empire by doing something pretty obvious, but doing it to such a degree that the clothing industry had to take notice. My company single-handedly changed how today's clothing is designed to accommodate technology. The North Face, Under Armour, Nautica, Burton, Polo Ralph Lauren and others have all licensed my clothing-related patent.

Fashion may come and go, but I was rethinking clothing from the inside out, one pocket at a time. My superhero alter ego could be Pocket Man, but in reality, that's just who I am all the time. If I have a superpower, it's passion: for promotion, for great customer service and for creating the absolute best pockets in the history of humankind.

I've grown my company from a simple idea to a massively multi-million dollar brand that has fans all over the world. Travelers, news correspondents, photographers, tech influencers, authors, special ops, commuters and just about everyone who has a SCOTTeVEST product swears by them. I've been able to travel the world and meet in person with thousands of fans (in the true sense of the word... they are fanatics). Among them are celebrities, media influencers, and at least half of the billionaires in the US. Seriously. (Google "Allen and Company SCOTTeVEST")

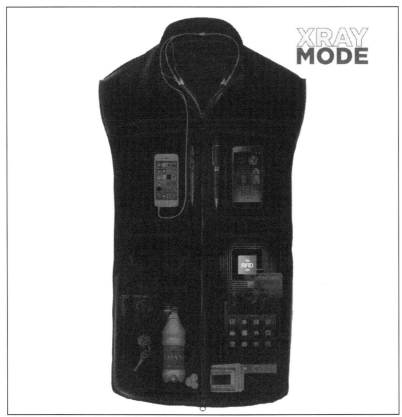

SCOTTeVEST products – like this flagship RFID Travel Vest – contain dozens of pockets to carry electronics and travel essentials. Since most of the features are hidden, we use x-ray imagery to show the inner workings. The difference is inside.

Why? Because I wasn't afraid to promote myself... passionately.

How This Book Works

- It's a book. Just freakin' read it. In all seriousness, there'll be stories, there'll be anecdotes, but this isn't going to be overly complex. If I'm telling a story and you don't know where it's going, keep reading. It's there for a reason.

- Here's a second bullet because the first one looked lonely.

P.S. Every story is true, but some are shortened to make a point, or so you wouldn't fall asleep.

P.P.S. There are links strewn throughout the book, but I put them in footnotes where possible. Consider this the world's first dual-screen printed book.

P.P.P.S. I don't swear gratuitously, but this book would not be rated PG. If it makes you feel better, I was actually quoted swearing by the *Wall Street Journal*.*

P.P.P.P.S. I started to write this book to get on major media talk shows like *Fallon, Kimmel, The Daily Show*, and *Colbert's* show. Even though my reasons for creating the book have evolved, appearing on *Colbert* or these other shows is still a major goal. Free pockets for life* if you can make that happen.

---

* Check it out at www.scottevest.com/wsjbleep
* No restrictions apply. If you get me on these major shows, you will have pockets for life. I'm talking hundreds of pockets in dozens of garments. Not kidding.

Chapter 1
Zero to Sixty

I've been obsessed with speed ever since I was a kid.

First, it was go-karts. Now, I race real cars. But speed isn't just about going fast down a track for me. I think fast, move fast and work fast.

I always have the newest and fastest gadgets, and I live my life as if I'm sprinting from the moment I get up in the morning until I fall asleep at night. My shrink has said I'm like a bulldozer with rocket fuel, and my employees, the people I pass, and just about everyone I come into contact with would agree.

Going fast, gadgets, cars, watches, poodles... maybe I haven't changed very much since I was a kid. Back then, I liked to think of myself as a James Bond wannabe, and I still do.

The cars have gotten better, and I've driven Porsches, Ferraris, Lamborghinis and more on real race tracks up to 150 miles per hour. For our international friends on the metric system, that's really freakin' fast. That's blinking fast.

I'm not a reckless road driver, but let's just say I'm on a first name basis with the traffic cops in my town. They seem to always be around whenever I turn north onto route 75 and head down the long, open stretch of road toward the Sawtooth Mountains in the distance. I have a 1990 Porsche 911, a 2006 Cayenne S Turbo, a 1974 BMW 3.0cs, a 1970 VW Westfalia Bus and a dirt bike. I buy cars for style, not status, and I only drive German these days, but I do have a deposit on an Alfa Romeo 4C.

Even my gadgets have gotten better. Remember all the crap they'd sell in the back of comic books? I would buy it all. The world's smallest radio. Next month's world's smallest radio. The transistor radio that looked like a UFO, the radio that ran from energy gathered from the earth's magnetic fields (yeah, that one didn't work). The mini TV, the pen light, the pen camera, the new model of the penlight, the Seiko watch with analog and digital times in 12 time zones when I never got more than three miles from my house.

Now I'm working from a MacBook Air, the newest iPhone and iPad, I have about 10 TVs in two bedrooms and I'm always trying to find the best, fastest, productivity-enhancing apps. I spend much of my day communicating through email, and I'm always looking for ways to optimize and manage the hundreds of threads I participate in each day.

I supported my gadget habit in my formative years with a paper route through the mean streets of Cincinnati (well, a suburb of Cincinnati). I was a paperboy, a dishwasher, a bus boy, a waiter... I even guessed weights at an amusement park one summer.

While I wouldn't say that I work today just to keep buying gadgets, they're a big part of who I am and how I work. They enhance my capabilities as a business owner, leader and promoter. In fact, I consider technology to be an absolutely vital part of running any business today. Technology and gadgets are a huge part of how I'm able to leverage media to grow my company.

Speed – working fast and moving fast – is at the core of who I am as a successful businessperson and passionate promoter.

My Career Path at 11

"I was born a poor black child. I remember the days, sittin' on the porch with my family...."

Ok, so that clearly wasn't my life. It's the opening lines from the Steve Martin movie *The Jerk*, and in all seriousness, there are a haunting number of parallels between my life and that movie. Even the fact that he worked at a carnival and invents such an obvious product hits home. See it if you haven't; it's hilarious.

> Another Steve Martin connection: he wears a SCOTTeVEST in his movie about birding *The Big Year*.

I actually grew up as a middle class Jewish kid in Philadelphia before my family moved to Ohio. Even though we lived most of my childhood in the Midwest, I never really lost my East Coast edge. Being the only boy born to my Jewish family, there were only a few choices for a career, and my career choice was a topic of conversation from the time I could dress myself in the morning. The natural choice would be to go into my father's business, but he owned a cemetery... and that's even worse than it sounds.

We never had a good relationship, and that became both a stumbling block and a motivator as I got older and found my way in the world. My father often berated me that I would drive his cemetery business into the ground if I ever took it over. Even worse, the irony of that statement was completely lost on him.

So that left only two clear choices: doctor or lawyer. Even then, I was very creative and after I won an art contest, I thought I might want to be artist. That wasn't one of the two choices... so it wasn't one of the two choices. The thought of me becoming an artist scared my mom, so she suggested that because architects draw, architecture could be a backup plan if I wanted to be creative. It was a stretch. Since I couldn't stand the sight of blood, the law started to look like the ~~best~~ only option.

It was made clear to me that pro race car driver and pro wrestler were only childhood dreams, and it would need to be the law.

> Irony of ironies: the kid who could only dress himself in Garaminals and wasn't allowed to do anything creative with his life is now effectively a fashion designer. Go figure.

Learning My Lessons

Some of the most important lessons I learned about life and business as a kid came to me through my dad. Just not in the way you think.

No one ever taught me how to succeed. In my earliest days, I learned a lot from my father. At least Charles Barkley announced that he was not a role model; I had to figure out my dad wasn't one all by myself.

He was a major negative influence on me, but eventually I turned it around and learned to use my desire to prove him wrong as a motivator. I grew up with an Ivy League education in getting my ass kicked, and my spirit stomped, both thanks to my dad, who told me I wouldn't amount to much. I believed him at the time, but a big part of who I am came through the process of beating his expectations of me.

My favorite quote from him was, "I resent you for all the opportunities that I have provided to you that were never provided to me." He made it clear that he wanted me to feel bad about that, and at the time it worked. I later learned that fathers are supposed to give their children opportunities to make them more confident and better, but I got the opposite treatment.

Circa 1974, Cincinnati

He also gave me an amazing gift of luggage, or more to the point, some baggage. Emotional, of course, and centered around the concept of laziness. My dad had one aspiration in life: to retire.

To him, the sign of a successful businessman was being able to retire early. In fact, the earlier the better. Perhaps I took that too much to heart as a 12 year old with my sights set on retirement, and I adopted a very lazy attitude. I aspired to be lazy.

Circa 1987, OSU Columbus Ohio graduation

Even though I was a lazy kid, my mom knew that I was smart. She was ahead of her time, and didn't take what the teachers and

21

even the results on paper said about me. She never doubted me, never believed I was "average at best" but it didn't sink in. When I was 13 or 14, she had me take an IQ test, and I scored 131 on it, aka I did really well (140 is considered genius level). It confirmed for her what she knew all along... I had a brain. It also planted a seed in me that didn't grow until I was in law school:

Lazy isn't something to aspire to.*

* That's a dangling participle. Get over it.

Pretty simple, huh? But learning that meant I would go against the core, driving, motivating force in my father's life. It was worth the fight, and that fight is the fire that lets me put it all on the line.

Rebel, Rebel

In the end, it would be rebelling against my dad that pushed me the hardest. I didn't start realizing how manipulative he was until I reached High School.

One summer, I broke the pattern of boring jobs that all my friends had, like bagging groceries and pumping gas, to go work at an amusement park. No, I wasn't a carnie. I also wasn't a rollercoaster tester or a bumper car referee. I didn't get the job of bikini inspector, but I came pretty damn close: I was hired to guess the ages and weights of parkgoers at King's Island outside of Cincinnati, Ohio.

It was actually a pretty damn cool job for a 16 year old. Not only was I being paid to check out girls and talk to them over a loudspeaker (yeah, yeah, and guys too), but I could make good money doing it. I wasn't just trying to strike up a conversation. I had a reason - a business reason - to do it.

On top of it all, if you worked through the whole summer and weekends, you would get a major bonus at the end: 25 cents extra for every hour you worked all summer. Not chump change when gas cost $1.25 a gallon (sorry metric people, you need to Google the conversion).

In the midst of my excitement over the summer job I landed, I made one major mistake. I told my dad.

About halfway through the summer, my father announced that I had to quit my job and help him with his business. No more fun, no bonus. He didn't tell me what he needed help with, but for a 16 year old, going from working at an amusement park to working at a cemetery was like... well, the reality was better than any metaphor.

It caused arguments. It caused fights. Ultimately, I stood my ground and didn't quit working at the amusement park. I didn't go to work for my dad. He gave me shit about it every day through the end of August, but I sucked it up. I wasn't going to let him win.

At the end of the summer after I got my bonus he told me something with a smirk: it was a test of loyalty to him. When he saw how much fun I was having, he wanted to see if I would give it up for him.

Thankfully, that wouldn't be the last time I disappointed him.

Positive or negative, finding a motivation that moves you at your core is vital. Sometimes, passion hurts.

My First Invention

The day I moved myself into college at The Ohio State University was as big an experience for me as any other kid away from home for the first time, and it wasn't because I was moving into a suite with 15 other guys.

Of course, I came bearing gadgets - a Sony Walkman, my Atari 2600, a clunky word processor - and I eventually was the guy who introduced the VCR to my frat house. I even had a copy of *Ferris Bueller's Day Off* (my favorite movie) and some porn. It felt like the opening scene to *2001: A Space Odyssey* when the monkeys first see the monolith that changes the course of their lives forever… just imagine how popular I was in a frat house!

Like most college kids, I had no idea what I wanted to study. Unlike most college kids, I was able to invent my own major: Entrepreneurship.

I'm sure I wasn't the first to come up with the idea, but I saw it through, and it was actually not that difficult. I found an open-minded Dean, did my research, put together a solid proposal and presented it. His objections and questions only sharpened my thinking.

"Why not just become a business major? Why don't you become a marketing major?"

To me, you study business to join an established business, not to start one. Marketing is a big piece of the pie, but it doesn't tell you how to start something from scratch. After about an hour of conversation, he was convinced, and the process convinced me even more: I was going to become an entrepreneur.

There was one entrepreneurship class already established at OSU, but it was more about the psychology of entrepreneurs, and not really about how to become one. I went through the course directories, spoke to professors, and was able to create a list of classes that would round out my new major.

It was unique at the time, but now it seems like just about every school has some version of this major, and not just University of Phoenix. I liked to push the envelope, and if there's room to do something different, why would I NOT take advantage of that? It's like air always filling a vacuum.

My favorite parts were always the practical exercises where we had to develop a new idea, create a plan to make it real and present it. I developed a subscription flower delivery service for cemeteries, where flowers would be automatically delivered each month, but my frustration with school was that at the end of the day, it was all just on paper.

It was like playing Monopoly instead of creating something in the real world. I wasn't able to move fast enough just sticking to theoretical examples. It was time for something more.

You can learn more from a day of doing than you can from a week of thinking.

Buckeyes and Beefcakes

When I was in college, there was an immensely popular collegiate calendar called *The Men of USC*. If you're a college sports fan, you already know that USC and OSU are rivals, so guess what I did?

I hope you guessed that I created a "Men of Ohio State University" calendar. If not, where did you think I was going with this?

Circa 1987, OSU

Anyway, the Men of OSU calendar was a great idea and everyone loved it... except for OSU. (Since this was the late 80s, it would be entirely appropriate to insert a record scratch sound effect there.)

Apparently, the school officials didn't like the idea of being associated with shirtless guys, and they certainly didn't like the idea of me and a couple of my frat brothers making money off the name of their school.

Shit.

But that wasn't going to stop me. The idea had too much potential, it was too immediate to ignore. Now was the time, and I was the guy to do it. Over, under, around or through... I was going to find a way. And I did.

In fact, I embraced the controversy. I relished it, I told people about it and I used it as a vehicle to get the word out about the calendar in a way that only controversy can do. "Did you hear about the student that might get sued by the school over a calendar?" It was a golden opportunity.

Before the calendar went to print, the name became the *Buckeye Men's Calendar*. Our sports teams are the Buckeyes, but the University doesn't own the name. It said the same thing, but in a way that everyone could live with. In retrospect, putting Buckeye in the name was even better, but the controversy generated by getting there made the calendar infamous around campus before it was even available.

It wasn't just the controversy that led to buzz and sales. It wasn't just the rivalry with USC. It wasn't even the pictures of half-naked dudes, school pride or that a portion of the proceeds went to benefit the OSU alumni foundation. The success came because I used facebook to choose the models. In 1987.

Social Media 1.0

No, I don't mean Facebook.com... it was 1987! I used the facebook, the book that everyone who went to college knows about, the book that shows a photo of every student with their name under it. This was the best part of the whole calendar idea. You may know the concept of Facebook was also based on the same type of campus "facebook."

I didn't pick the absolute best-looking guys. I chose the most popular guys. I polled the sororities to figure out who I should use (added benefit: I got a few phone numbers, too). I found men who were the life of every frat party and always had an audience, and I gave them something to talk to their audience about: my calendar. All of their friends bought calendars to support them, and it made the calendar and the Images Calendar Line a runaway success.

We photographed a football player in front of the stadium as an F.U. to OSU. We sold ads to bars to sponsor days for most of the year, announcing a ladies night at this bar or that bar, drink specials and things like that. The bars were our customers because we brought them customers. Beyond just the photos, the deals and events in the calendar made it relevant the whole year.

I did press releases and got a lot of media coverage; not just in the student papers. This was when I learned to use the media, and I have done it ever since. I was even interviewed on TV*.

---

* www.scottevest.com/calendar to watch.

27

The stories were not just about the calendar, but about college students starting a business. The fact that OSU tried to shut us down was just fuel for the fire.

This was analog social media, and I discovered I was good at it. The more emotionally invested someone is in your cause, your idea, your business, your product, or just you... the more they will want you to succeed and help you do it. That's the real power of social media, regardless of the tools you use to do it.

People will promote things when they participate in them. I create opportunities for that to happen.

People Are Dying to Get in There

The calendar business came to a close as graduation approached. It was a great idea and a solid start, but there were some problems. We considered doing a women's version with a bar sponsoring the whole thing, but I didn't like the way the bar owner treated women, so I backed out. Some disagreements with my frat brothers who worked on the calendar with me were the final nails in the coffin. That experience ultimately soured me on the idea of ever taking on business partners or having to answer to investors or a boss. Oh, and speaking of coffins...

After college, my father wanted me to go into the family line of work and to become a traveling cemetery salesman. More specifically, he tricked me into it by toasting to my future success at a family holiday gathering. As if that wasn't enough, there was a catch: I wasn't even going to work for his company. I was being "traded" to other cemetery companies to learn the ropes like ~~the world's lowest paid professional athlete~~ a scrawny, unwanted little leaguer.

At 21 years old, ink still wet on my diploma, he sent me to Baltimore, Maryland. It's called the Charm City, but I didn't get to see any of the charming parts, and I really didn't have anywhere to live until I was able to stay with my cousins. It didn't last more than a month, and I moved on to my next rotation in a different city, but the story was always the same.

This is how it worked:

- **The job**: sell cemetery plots.

- **The training**: twenty minutes on the job.

- **The techniques:** cold call and knock on doors.

- **The pitch (three per night):** "Do you have a family?... How long have you been in the community?... Congratulations! You won a $500 cemetery plot. Yes, really! I just need to come by to get your information and fill out some paperwork. How about six o'clock tonight?" They actually did all "win" ONE $500 plot, but who wants to be buried alone? That's where the payment plan for additional plots came in, not to mention the extra costs for the casket, burial services, etc....

- **The pay:** all on commission... no sales, no pay.

29

- **The territory:** parts of cities where I would be more likely to need a cemetery plot than to sell one.

Even though I hated it and had no passion for it, I felt like I had to beat my dad at his own game. In the end, I closed just one sale in a couple months, and dealing with the rejection was hard.

I learned that I needed to believe in something to sell it. Now, I believe in me.

That's why I'm willing to go to the ends of the Earth to promote myself.

A New Low

Eventually, my dad called me home after recognizing I was not a great salesman. I became fairly successful working in his business, and I turned out to be a pretty good manager. I was even able to buy a small house, which was a cool thing for a young twenty-something to be able to do.

Things started to improve between us…

…and then my dad sold the family business out from under me. He sold it to a reputed mobster (who later died in a helicopter crash under mysterious circumstances), but there was no intimidation involved; this was all his idea.

I thought I was being groomed (well, more like put through the wringer) as training to learn what I would need to learn to take over the family legacy. I expected to be the "& Son" on the proverbial sign, even if in reality it turned out to be more like *Sanford & Son*. I guess I still held out some hope for repairing the relationship that had never been right in the first place.

I was devastated. I wound up continuing to work with the new owners during the transition period, which was for less than a year, but there was nothing waiting for me on the other end.

It was time for me to make a move, and that move was to go to law school. My father threatened to not help me pay for it, but he ultimately gave into pressure from mom.

I wasn't going to take anything else from my Father. Never again.

Time to Face the Music

From the first time I turned away from looking at a scraped knee and made a career in medicine impossible, I was on the path to law school. Like it or not. Case Western Reserve Law, here I come....

My problem with becoming a lawyer was I was jaded against them. When I was a kid, my father lost a lawsuit and blamed lawyers. Not just THE lawyers, or those lawyers, but the entire justice system. It made an impression on me, even though I didn't know at the time that almost ALL of the impressions my father made on me were negative. I went to law school because I was lost, the family business was sold and law school was the clearest path forward.

Ultimately, I wanted to be something and make my mom proud.

circa 1987, OSU graduation

Looking back, I never intended to be a lawyer even when I was in law school. My intention had been to call other lawyers to task, to hold them accountable and to make my place in the legal

31

world as a malpractice lawyer suing other lawyers. Sounds pretty heroic, right?

But a funny thing happened on the way to graduation. I did well. Really well. I had never been a good student, and more importantly, I never thought of myself as one. I even had the grades to back that up.

I decided to apply myself in law school and not to follow the frat boy lifestyle I embraced in college. I decided to do (most) of the reading, to do all the writing, to study my ass off and to give a shit. In fact, I gave all I had. I did it for my mom. I did it because I found out my mom was dying. ALS. She was diagnosed one week after I started and died December of the following year with me at her side.

Even though she was gone before I was done with school, my resolve never wavered because I had a bigger purpose in my life. I burned through my laziness and I liked how it felt. I sent all my grades - every single one of my grades as I got tests and papers back - to a law firm until they granted me the summer internship I needed. I persisted because I knew my mom would have been proud that I did.

I think about her a lot. Even today, especially today.

And Then I Was A Lawyer

Is it just me, or do you notice everyone in the room tense up when they find out someone in their midst is a lawyer? Welcome to the rest of my life.

Being a lawyer is the opposite of being an entrepreneur. When you are a lawyer, it defines who you are, what you do, when you do it and who you answer to. My new career required me to behave in a way that was almost exactly opposite my natural inclinations:

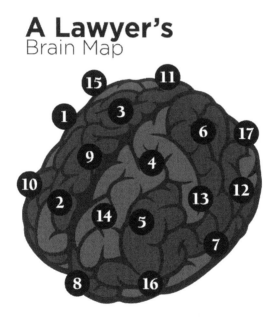

1. Billable hours
2. What's for lunch?
3. Billable hours
4. Billable hours
5. Did I write down my billable hours?
6. How can I get more billable hours?
7. Sex.
8. ~~Can sex be considered billable hours?~~ Ask accountant, bill for time with accountant.
9. ~~Is my work good enough to bill for?~~ It doesn't really matter.

10. I need to remember my billable hours and go back and write them down.
11. ~~Independent thinking.~~
12. Think about every scenario that could happen, no matter how unlikely. Wake up in the middle of the night when you remember you missed something. All billable.
13. I could be fired for a typo.
14. I need to be seen. Face-time Fridays. All billable.
15. Get bigger clients who don't review their bills closely.
16. How can I bill my clients for playing Solitaire?
17. Does a *siesta* count toward billable hours?

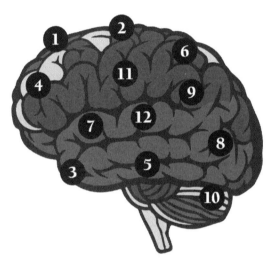

1. How can I improve this?
2. Why is this taking so long?
3. There has to be a better way.
4. What's for lunch?
5. Faster faster faster.
6. What's the point of doing it this way just because it had been done this way in the past?
7. Sex.
8. Time isn't the only thing I can sell, and it certainly isn't the best.
9. I need to be my own mentor and seek my own training.
10. Follow-up fast and often.
11. Time sheets are prison bars, and usually at least part fiction.
12. **I must be a master of my own time.**

I get more done because I streamline my thinking.

Getting Turned On

Discovering the significant power I had to apply myself and get things done was ultimately a blessing and a curse in law school. Once the lightbulb clicked on, I used it. I did TOO well in my classes. I graduated in 1992 *Summa Cum Laude* with a 3.93 GPA from Case Western Reserve Law School and was 6th in my class of over 200 students.

I was capable of being the superhero anti-lawyer I envisioned, and doing it really well. But I did too well in law school. I received offers from some of the top law firms in the country and I took one. I wasn't going to be an anti-lawyer, I was going to be a lawyer. Just a lawyer. What do you do when you're just getting out of school and faced with a great opportunity? Yeah, that's what I did. So sue me. But don't really, because I'm a lawyer.

Rudnick & Wolfe (which later merged to become DLA Piper with over 4,200 lawyers) is now one of the largest law firms in the world, and they wanted me. It was a victory, and I knew my mom would have been proud of this achievement. I had the grades, I had the drive, and they were giving me a golden opportunity. I was psyched, I was pumped. I was going to be a deal maker, running with the big dogs. I was going to fly around the country in private jets with the movers, shakers and movers-and-shakers. Lunch with CEOs, dinner with Presidents. I was going to get that Porsche. In fact, they should just give me the keys on my first day.

And then, when the champagne was flowing - SNAP - welcome back to reality. I was brought in to be the lowest of the low, a grunt, an I-dotter, a T-crosser. I aced my exams, graduated at the top of my class, and this is where they put me? In insurance litigation, which was the worst type of law that I could be forced to practice.

If I did that well in school, where do they put the people who graduate at the bottom of the class? This was NEVER where I thought I would wind up. The fact that I was making a decent living as a recent grad was my only comfort, but the Porsche I envisioned? Not even close.

35

I convinced myself the situation was OK for now. I continued to bill 200+ hours per month myself, and I was consistently at the top of my "class" in the firm. I made a lot of money for the firm, and I had a future there. They would make me a Junior Partner in about… seven years? Seven years? Really?

The walls were closing in on me and my law career.

It's Not the Final Straw that Breaks the Camel's Back. It's the First 9,999 Straws.

I was sitting in my office at one of the most prestigious law firms in the world, and instead of doing my work - my all important billable hours - I found myself playing Solitaire on my computer. And then again, and again. And again. And again. I was becoming addicted to Solitaire, and it made me feel like a shit. I realized something very important:

The antithesis of freedom is to need to account for your time in 1/10th hour increments. When your time is not your own, you are not free.

Even as a young lawyer in 1993, my firm was billing me out at $275 per hour. My six minutes were worth $27.50. Are your six minutes worth that? Mine weren't.

There are many people in the world who are unhappy with their jobs and looking to make the leap into entrepreneurship the way I did. A lot of people have asked me when I decided that I had to stop being a lawyer. Well, it was right at that moment.

Once you become more enamored with playing Solitaire than with work, you're done. Pack up, go home, find a new line of work. I "hit rock bottom" when I played 3 hours of Solitaire in one day and had to write down 8 hours of billable time. My procrastination turned into a late night work frenzy making up the time, and it brought back a flood of fear that I was reverting into my lazy, pre-Law School self.

Time for a change. Now. As in **right now**.

One legitimate path for a lawyer at a large firm to take is to go in-house and work for a client. I laid everything out on the table and asked the managing partner of my firm Lee Miller if he would help me make some contacts. I was clear that I intended to leave the firm before my work slipped. He is still the managing partner and the biggest bigwig there 20 years later.

I had painted myself into a corner for a reason. No turning back now.

Painting Myself Into Corners: I'm always painting myself into corners, and that's a good thing. In my case, it shows a level of self-understanding. I need to paint myself into corners. I need to burn bridges behind me. I even did it when I proposed to my wife Laura in July of 1995 after knowing her for a few years, and dating her for about 9 months.

I proposed while in a park on a picnic in Chicago. I was so nervous that I put a card in the picnic basket at the bottom with the inscription "Will you marry me?"

I left it there to force me to ask the "question" since I knew without it I would likely wuss out. Well, after 2 hours in the oddly cold/windy Chicago afternoon, with rain about to pour, while stalling, Laura finally was fed up and ready to go home when she saw the card and asked what it was for. I replied, and this is a direct quote: "It's a card asking you to marry me as I'm too scared to do it myself" and with that I flung the card at her. Fortunately for me she said yes.

Little did I know that Laura would truly make me the happiest and luckiest man alive, even to this day, and every day more happy and lucky.

For the record, I considered proposing to Laura at the Grateful Dead concert at Soldier Field we were planning to go to the next day instead of the park, but thought it was not romantic enough. It was my first Dead concert, and it happened to be their last one. Laura told me she would have much preferred being proposed to at a Grateful Dead concert rather than some lame attempt to be romantic. All the more reason I'm the luckiest man alive.

The next weeks at the law firm were pretty torturous, but there was a light at the end of the tunnel... a few, actually. I interviewed with a company to become their in-house counsel. Then another. Then another. My resume and contacts were able to open doors, but I couldn't close the deal and it began to freak me out.

One day, I got a call from a recruiter, and I knew it would be the big break I had been waiting for, the one I deserved. "There may be an opportunity for you" rang in my ears when I heard their voicemail, and I couldn't call them back fast enough. Was it a job with a big client? Was it one of the dozens of companies I applied to, reaching out to me through a recruiter?

No. It was the unimaginable.

I was being recruited to be a corporate lawyer again. Even worse, it was to work for another major law firm, the competition, the enemy... Katten Muchin & Zavis (known as KMZ at the time, a collection of three particularly oddly named Jewish dudes). Just taking the interview could have been career suicide if my current firm found out, but I had already walked the plank by this point, gaining speed toward the ground.

I went over to the dark side and took the offer.

Darkest Before Dawn

There were no birds singing. No rainbows. No reprieve. It was SSDJ (Same Shit, Different Job).

I realized that I didn't need a fresh start. I needed a way out, and I still did. This was a really dark time for me because I lost respect for myself. I just didn't like the level of work I was doing at my new firm KMZ and "survival" is only a good motivator for so long. I burned a bridge at my old firm DLA Piper, but that turned out to be a great thing; I just didn't realize it yet.

I don't know if I believe in a soul, but my new job was beating the shit out of mine on a daily basis. I had spent successive months working and billing more than 250 hours (instead of 200 as at my previous firm) and it was tearing me apart. I was working 20% longer hours for the same pay as before. It felt like Groundhog Day.

My wife Laura told me that I sat bolt upright in bed one night, screaming "Miserable, miserable, no end in sight," then rolled over and went back to sleep. I don't recall that happening at all, but I took it as a sign that if I didn't do something to take care of myself, my soul, my guts, then there was no way back.

Was I in a race against unhappiness? death? old age? a raise that would make me rethink whether it was really that bad? You've been there, right? Feeling like you're in a fight against unseen forces, but not really knowing what you're facing. I figured it out, though. I realized I was in a race against mediocrity and that:

If you accept mediocrity in any form for long enough, you become mediocre. Period.

I could imagine vividly what the mediocre version of me would look like. He was a horrifying cliche, a caricature of my deepest concerns and worst tendencies. We had the same face, but he had three more chins and looked pasty because he only got one week of sun every year during his vacation.

He was sixty pounds overweight and he didn't carry it well. He made decent money - about $150K per year - but he worked 70 hours per week as "of counsel" at a law firm and hated every minute of it. It was a dead-end job and he did it well enough to fly under the radar whenever personnel were discussed by management. He gamed the system to make sure that he was never anything more than perfectly average, and the machinations to make that happen were the most amusing part of his day.

His billable hours were solid, but he spent as much time rounding them up as he did being productive. Laura divorced him after a couple years. He remarried a nice Jewish girl, had a bunch of kids and watched as she steadily became her mother, pound by pound, nag by nag. She was afraid of dogs, and he would never own one again.

Always in a bad mood, he burned every bridge... not just the ones to motivate him to move forward, but the ones he could have used, too. His first sip of alcohol came before work in the mornings, and it was far from his last sip of the day.

39

True story about how supportive Laura is: I have, on several occasions, seriously suggested changing my last name from "Jordan" to "Vest." My middle name is Elliot. Therefore, my name would be Scott E. Vest. She told me that if I did that, a) it had to be for PR purposes, and b) she would change her last name to Gordon instead of Jordan, since she prefers it as a nod to Commissioner Gordon from Batman. So... should I change my name?

Let me know what you think about it on my Facebook page: www.facebook.com/sevscottjordan

Delaying the Inevitable

After about 10 months, I didn't find a way out, but a way out found me. I received a call from a recruiter about a dream job as corporate counsel at a publicly traded company. The offer was to be the Associate General Counsel of Brookdale Living Communities, and I couldn't say yes fast enough. Even the title sounded like a promotion. They hired me as quickly as I could get out of my old job, but it turned out to be more like working at a law firm than I ever expected.

Remember how much I hate timesheets and tracking billable hours? In part, I took the Brookdale job at a company (not a law firm) to get away from ever needing to keep track of my time again. On my first day - my first freaking day – billable hours became a mandatory part of my job description. Surprise! Even better, I found out during my first annual review that no one looked at my timesheets even once.

I was out of there. I started to worry that three jobs in two years on one resume didn't add up to a good impression.

A few months later, an opportunity fell into my lap. One of the senior execs at Brookdale - Nigel Albert Rathbone Pemberton-Buckley IV or something equally ridiculous - had left the company and started a startup (which is what you do with startups) called Next50.com. I helped them raise $3 million in funding, and they made me a good offer with options and a salary. To this day, I can't grasp who thought it was a good enough company to fund, but that wasn't important at the time.

I had the chance to be an entrepreneur. This was going to be my life.

Next50.com

Next50 was intended to be an online community for seniors, sort of like a Facebook for older people. Even before I started there, I recognized that the revenue model was idiotic (because there was none). But I knew exactly how they could create one and they were offering me an equity stake in the venture.

The founders originally wanted to name it Seniors On Line, but when I pointed out that spelled S.O.L. they looked for other options. I suggested Next50, and it stuck.

I saw the potential in the idea, and it jazzed me that I could play a role in shaping this company into something valuable and cool. It was 1999 and not having a revenue model was apparently not enough to stop them from getting funding. (Or to stop anyone and everyone else from getting funding, for that matter.)

I was a fountain of marketing ideas, and every one of them would bring in revenue. I could clearly see the potential of this startup with the right leadership, and I wanted in. It was going to be like my calendar venture, but with more wrinkles and less exposed skin.

The biggest downside to Next50 was that I had to commute to Princeton, NJ from Chicago, and I only got to spend weekends at home. Well, that and my boss was a dick... a huge one. You know the kind. And he made it very clear they were not interested in my revenue ideas, my marketing ideas, or any of my ideas... this startup did not need to generate any revenue yet.

Huh? What were they waiting for? Isn't that the reason why people start a business and other people invest in that business?

He summed it up by saying, "The best thing about these internet companies is that no one cares about revenue." It was an unfortunate mentality that was running rampant at the time. Revenue, profitability, and accountability did not matter at all. That's why the dot-com bubble burst in 2000.

That's when I learned how startups operate with OPM (Other People's Money). It's a mindset that still pisses me off to this day, and it's one I vowed never to participate in. I've made good on my promise with SCOTTeVEST: we have always been 100% self-funded, profitable, and cash-flow positive. It's not easy to do, but certainly not impossible when you give yourself no other choice.

When you self-fund, you can grow or die... but make sure you don't die growing. It's a balance to keep in mind when you don't have the safety net of OPM. Self-funding from cash flow on an inventory basis, on a business-to-business (B2B) model where you can't predict your demand makes *how* you grow all the more vital vs. a funded company. It can sink you if you aren't careful.

Make a Move

One positive of all that flying back and forth is that it gave me time to think. I still think best while I'm moving: traveling, racing Porsches, skiing, walking the poodles, or just bouncing off the walls in the office. I've been accurately described as a bulldozer with rocket fuel, and that description fit me even then. Work + speed = Scott. Because I traveled constantly for this job, I always had my gadgets in tow:

- Sony VAIO laptop and charger;
- Motorola StarTAC phone and charger;
- Sony voice recorder and spare batteries;
- Palm Pilot and wires to connect it to my phone;
- Sony DiscMan, CDs, headphones and spare batteries;
- More batteries. Everything needed batteries.
- Cords, cords and more cords. Everything had a different adapter, battery connector and interface. There was no standardized micro-USB-universal-plugs at the time.

Traveling sucked, even in 2000 before the TSA was formed, and very few people were carrying the amount of electronics I was on an almost daily basis. I was a fanny pack and man purse poster child, and looking back at photos, I'm realizing how much I started to look like the vision of the mediocre me that made me lose sleep at night.

I worked in a business casual environment, and even a nice sport jacket can be transformed into a bulky-looking mess when it doesn't have appropriate pockets for your stuff. Running through the office I almost lost an ear when my headphone wire caught on a door knob and yanked me like a helpless salmon being snatched from a stream. It was an intense pain I would remember later, and second only to looking like this:

43

Circa 1994, Marrakech

While the job was unfulfilling, that weekly commute became the genesis for the idea behind SCOTTeVEST. It cemented in me the pain of traveling with all the stuff that I wanted to carry, and the inconvenience of it all. I quit the job at Next50 at the end of summer 2000 because the weekly trips were killing me. I knew I had to do it. I had started playing Solitaire again. I started to take private law clients while at work. The worst part was that all my wasted time had no effect on the business because nothing productive or revenue-centric was happening anyway.

It was clear that things were not going to get any better, and they certainly weren't headed toward anywhere good with leadership like that. I was lost again, and trying to find myself. I went on interview after interview to no avail. I used personal connections to get close to one of the most powerful figures in Chicago insurance, and was a shoo-in for a job. Then the word on the street was that he was under investigation by the Feds. Later, he was indicted (Mickey Segal - look it up.)

I'm absolutely allergic to shady dealings, so I needed another path, and fear sunk in. I still didn't know where to leap, and that ground far below was intimidating to the point of paralysis.

Then it hit me. It wasn't a lightbulb moment...more like a sledgehammer: after Next50, I could only be a lawyer. I was stuck. Marooned.

This was my first "business" experience working for anything other than a law firm, and I still had only done lawyer work. There wasn't even a lot of that to do at a startup. I began to think that this was going to be the path of the rest of my life.

It was a death sentence to someone who could never picture himself as a lawyer. It was surrendering my identity to be the thing I hated and feared most. It was as if I was wearing the scarlet letter, and that letter was L. For lawyer. (I really hope you figured that out on your own.)

I had burned all my bridges; I only had one move other than resigning myself to being the mediocre me I dreaded. I had to start a company... and it was the best thing I ever did.

At first, it was fear holding me back. Fear of failure, fear of doing... well, I had no idea what I would do. And then, eventually, I knew what I would do... and I still held back. It took the encouragement of Laura to break free, to stop looking, and to start leaping.

Initial In-vest-ment

It was November of 2000, and if you've ever been to Chicago anywhere near winter, you know it starts to get pretty raw. Even though I left Next50 in August, I was still doing some work for them through the fall to pay bills while I figured out what I was going to do next. It was tough, but at least I got to work from home. I found myself going on a lot of long walks and hikes with Laura in Palos Park near Chicago, and I needed the time to think. Every other day I would pitch her with another business idea to get her reactions and input.

Then, SCOTTeVEST started with a lightbulb moment.

Ok, so it wasn't a blinding flash, more like a weak flicker that grew brighter and brighter as I worked through all the details. But it was the genesis of something great.

For years - for my whole life - I had been a gadget guy, as you know. And for just as long as I was collecting and using gadgets, I've had to carry them around. When I was younger, backpacks were my go-to. In the 90s, fanny packs became about as socially acceptable as they have ever been (or ever will be). When I got married, gadget toting duties fell to Laura if she was carrying a bag and didn't want to been seen with me in public wearing a fanny pack.

I remember standing at the door of our house in Chicago, figuring out what gadgets I needed to bring with me for the day. I kept handing her more and more stuff until she said, "I'm not your personal Sherpa! Why don't you just design something to carry all your own shit around?"

It was a brilliant question, and that was all the flash I needed.

It got my gears turning. But what would it look like? I knew from all my commuting to New Jersey that a carry-on bag can be a pain to sift through when you're sitting in a seat, and I wasn't going to carry a totally separate bag just for my electronics.

Organization was key, and organization meant pockets. This was going to be something I could wear, not carry. People didn't need yet another bag to occupy their hands.

Old Navy had a national campaign to bring down vests back into style, and I thought a vest might be a good starting point as the core of something more extensive. It was, but theirs didn't have nearly enough pockets for the tons of things I carried. The sporting goods store had fishing vests, but they were as ugly as a fanny pack. Photo vests looked like fishing vests. Still, I bought a bunch and tested them out, learned what worked and what didn't.

With each test, with each vest, the common thread was clear: pockets are the key, but no one was doing them right. They were bulky and designed to carry things I would never carry. I needed pockets that would carry gadgets... pockets that were shaped and sized for the things that people carry all the time, such as cell phones and PDAs and batteries and wires.

I figured out a way to route the wires through the lining of the vest to get from a pocket up to the collar, which would eliminate the possibility of getting my cords caught on a doorknob and tearing off part of my ear. In fact, I could run headphone cords, fuel cell wires, external battery packs for charging devices, or even connect my DPC cord between my Palm and my StarTAC phone so I could essentially have dial-up internet through the cell service. What did it take to make this Personal Area Network aka PAN (as I named it)? Not much.

Yet again, I felt like Steve Martin in *The Jerk* when he invented the Opti-Grab eyeglasses with a nose brace to keep them from falling off your face when you look down. All I had to do was make a hole in a pocket, a hole near the collar and add something like a loop so the wire doesn't flop around. Why hadn't anyone thought of this before? Why hadn't EVERYONE? Surely, this had to be patented... it just seemed so obvious to me.

But it wasn't patented. Not yet. It was mine. This was going to be my patent, and this was going to be my company. If the Opti-Grab (fictional as it was) could catch on and make millions, so could this seemingly obvious idea. It was my "why didn't I think of that" moment, but I did think of it. This could be something I license to every single clothing company on Earth!

Now I was on fire. I had to get this from in my head to on my back. I bought every vest I could find as a reference, and the more I toyed with the concept, the more convinced I became that I was onto something.

Until I tried to make one.

On Pins and Needles

The Wright Brothers had a workshop. Nicola Tesla had a lab. Steve Wozniak had a garage.

They were all able to achieve great things because they were able to literally BUILD great things. I would be no different. But I was.

I had no idea how to sew. Not a button, not a hole, and certainly not a vest. This was just going to be a prototype, so no point in learning now, but I had to at least learn what needed to be done.

There was something like a small business advisor for new apparel brands at the Merchandise Mart in Chicago, so we made an appointment to get some advice on how to get started in the clothing manufacturing business. The woman we met with had been in the industry for decades, and she told me that we just needed to create a pattern! Even better, it would be super easy. About a half hour later, I was loaded up with all the advice (I thought) I would ever need about making clothing patterns.

Laura and I went to Fishman's Fabric Store on the south side of Chicago, picked up three yards of rough khaki fabric and a box of pins, and got down to business. This is where "super easy" fell apart. If I were making a normal vest, yeah, it might have been pretty easy. But I was tasked with creating a pattern for the most complicated garment you could make, short of an astronaut suit. I am not exaggerating about this. If you ever spend the twelve hours it takes to deconstruct a SCOTTeVEST, you'll understand. There are literally hundreds of individual pieces required.

Through the course of an afternoon, Laura and I almost got a divorce, right there on our living room floor. It was one of the four major fights we've ever had. I've never touched a clothing pattern ever again.

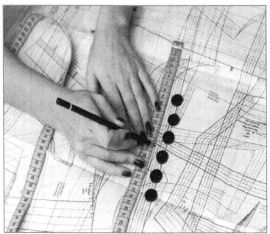
Pretty much the exact opposite of this

I was beyond frustrated, but it was also a lightbulb moment. I realized: I'm not a fashion designer and I'm not a seamstress. This attempt at crafting a pattern with no background and no clue really put me in a funk. I didn't want to be a fashion designer; I wanted to license this system to other brands. But I still needed something to prove the concept. I still needed **something** to sell while I applied for a patent.

There had to be a better way than sticking pins through fabric scraps in my apartment. I needed to hire a clothing designer to help me. Enter Susie Kruger.

We were introduced by a mutual contact, and I immediately hired her to make the first samples. It didn't take her long to create them, and she got most of the details right on the first try. They were my first and only samples, and they weren't perfect, but good enough to get started. I wanted to keep wearing them, playing with them, loading them up, but we were on a deadline: I needed to have vests in-hand by July, a little over six months away.

Turning on the Machine

I wasn't in a great place. I was feeling pretty desperate, but I was not all-in with "SCOTTeVEST" yet. I didn't even love the

49

name, but since we were really going to be more of a licensing and holding company, I didn't really care that it was awkward. "Scott's Electronics Vest" company was in officially in business, but I still had one foot on the ground and hadn't fully committed... I was still looking for jobs as a lawyer. The deciding factor would need to be whether I could jump-start this business and generate enough money for this to be my real job.

I had to promote my Personal Area Network. It could become the "Intel Inside" of clothing. I had to promote my product. I had to promote myself. There was no margin of error in my life, and no going back. I could only move forward, and I had to do it fast.

I started looking for every shortcut I could find to get myself in the right headspace-- hypnotherapy, personality testing, aptitude testing, self-medication, prescribed medication. All I learned was that I was a Myers-Briggs ENFJ, I was hard to hypnotize, Paxil was a joke, and I was able to fall asleep even taking the maximum dose of Ritalin. Basically, I didn't learn anything useful from those processes.

Deep inside, I just wanted to escape the lame version of the American dream, and I convinced myself there was only one way to succeed: the vest needed to be picked up by Sharper Image and Hammacher Schlemmer. As a gadget guy, it was like an artist trying to get into the Louvre. It would be a stretch, but if I pulled it off, I'd be set for life.

I had two precious samples in hand. After multiple follow-ups, Sharper Image finally replied that they didn't see the value in what I was offering. It just pissed me off enough to push harder... in fact, I printed it and tacked it to my wall. Hammacher was my sole target now, and I had an ace up my sleeve: I knew the landlord who owned their offices. I had enough of an "in." I just needed one toe in the door, which I got through a preliminary meeting to show off the vests. Now, they just had to get back to me and tell me if they wanted them.

Laura was away with her mom in Sun Valley, Idaho for a week of skiing, and I was home all alone. If you drew a chart of my emotional state from the day I was born until the day I die, this day in January 2001 would stand out as the lowest point of all.

I knew I needed help.

I was in my hypnotherapist Mark Oster's office for another soul searching trip down deep, deep inside my mind, when my phone rang. It was Hammacher (duh). In the middle of a session, I told Mark I had to pick it up. Either his services would no longer be needed, or he would need to talk me down, but either way... I had to take it right... freaking... now.

Up to this point, everyone I had talked to about SCOTTeVEST was either ecstatic about the idea or didn't get it at all. Literally, a 50/50 shot. If I knew it was going to be such a close call between the two sides, I would have actually kept score.

So which way would Hammacher Schlemmer fall? Were they calling to blow me off, or was this my shot? Would I be working for SCOTTeVEST or taking the next legal job that crossed my path?

Heads. They loved the concept and wanted to work out the details. Come in tomorrow, bring samples and a pen.

Everything changed in an instant. Every cloud lifted. I stopped searching for other jobs. I stopped needing intense therapy. I hit the jackpot. I jumped head first.

My hypnotherapist charged me for the full hour and declared me cured. It was a good day. It had been the worst day, and now it was the best day.

So much for rock bottom.

Heads

Samples in hand, I showed up for the follow-up meeting with their buyer. I was so passionate about the opportunity to present and go over the details of a deal that I didn't sleep the night before, and I didn't care. There were some new people in the room this time, so I ran through the pitch, I loaded and unloaded the pockets, put the vest on everyone and described how the Personal Area Network was a patent pending way to integrate wires into clothing, and would change the world of apparel forever.

At the time, I referred to the licensing end of the business as PAN-TECH, and would later rename it TEC-Technology Enabled Clothing®. TEC was more descriptive of the innovation, but regardless of what it was called, this would be a golden opportunity for Hammacher to get in on the ground floor of the future of clothing.

"The price? The price is fair based on the amount of unique features compared to other travel vests on the market: $159.99."

eVEST 1.0 beta, circa January 2001

"Oh, you mean the cost? Uhh... keystone? Oh, yes, the wholesale cost is keystone... 50% off the retail price."

"Delivery? How soon do you want them? I'll need to check with my factory before confirming delivery, but we're looking at July of this year. That is **really** fast for clothing made overseas, isn't it!"

I left there beaming from ear to ear. I was going to be in Hammacher Schlemmer.

Now I just needed to find a factory. Ohhhhh shit.

Made in China

If I didn't want my big break to break me in half, I needed to find a factory ASAP. I had intended all along to make SCOTTeVEST into a licensing company, but these Hammacher vests were going to be a proof of concept that would prove the concept all the way to the bank! If, you know, I could find a factory to make them in record time.

I reached out to everyone I knew who was even remotely connected to overseas sourcing. Kurt Gutfreund came through for me. He introduced me to KT Suh, an agent in Korea who worked closely with clothing factories in China. I had been concerned about "sweatshops" and the use of child labor when sourcing in China, but KT only worked with the cleanest, best operated factories. Even to this day, I have every new factory visited and documented by a third party inspector.

KT needed to see a sample to get me a price, and my self-imposed timeline to have vests in-hand by July meant there was a clock ticking. I didn't even know how long it would actually take to make them, but I knew we only had until July... so that's the longest it could be. To this day, I still work with KT.

Everything went to KT, and he got back to me after an excruciatingly long wait - $21.30 per unit plus duties and shipping - which I thought was fair. He said it was the most complicated garment he had ever seen or tried to construct. I knew what I had to spend, I took a gamble, and I placed an order for 3,000 vests. So much for needing to go to China if you want to do business there!

In between my introduction to KT and receiving a price from him, I had to become an expert in importing goods from overseas. It was confusing, but think of how many tens of thousands of businesses do it... if they could figure it out, so could I. I knew I had to think backwards from the goal and work out all the steps. A pain, but not hard. That's still how I approach problems today.

I left another message for the buyer at Hammacher with a status update: "Hi, just wanted to let you know that the factory confirmed they can meet the July delivery date I promised (more or less). Oh, and I still haven't received the countersigned paperwork back from you. Are there any problems?"

No problems, just silence. Which becomes a problem.

Tails

Showing up at the office of a major corporation unannounced should not be your opening move. But there is a point where it becomes your only move. It had been well over a month, and I had left no fewer than 15 voicemails for the buyer without any reply. Emails, too. I placed a $60,000 order for a product based on their commitment, and it wasn't just $60,000.

It was my money. It was almost all of my money.

The Hammacher deal seemed like fate. So was this a twist of fate? My stomach was twisted at least.

They let me in to see him, no problem. He had a box in his hand and was cleaning out his desk. Last day there.

He attempted a hand-off to the apparel buyer, but she was in the non-believing 50%.

The deal disappeared with him. Crushed. Defeated. Down.

More Coins

I was lost that day. If I hadn't painted myself into a corner, if I hadn't burned some bridges, I might have turned around. I might have started sending my resume to law firms and begging to get a job that paid. I might have been untrue to myself. But I couldn't.

When I invested most of my life savings into those vests, I crossed the point of no return. If there was no way back, I could only go forward. They were already in production. They were coming. They were coming soon. It was time to act.

In my down state, I calculated what I could make if I sold all the vests at keystone pricing (50% off retail). It wasn't much. It wasn't enough. I realized that I had given up the possibility of a $150K per year law job to be a pauper. Selling these vests wholesale was not going to cut it.

Months before, while developing the product, I also developed a website. In those days, your company was automatically pretty cool if it had a website, so it was an easy decision for me to have one built. While going through the list of what the site should include with my coder, he asked if I wanted it configured to let people place orders online. It would only cost me $500. At first I didn't want to bother, but then I said, "Sure."

Turns out, that casual "sure" is what saved me and got me on the right track.

Hammacher wasn't the end of the road, it was the beginning. Who needs catalogs and wholesale prices with 50%+ margins? I was going to keep the whole pie.

To this day, I'm convinced that keystone is the most popular wholesale pricing model because it's the easiest way for buyers, wholesalers, and retailers to do the math. If you pick up anything on the shelf at a store, and you can guess that the store probably paid 50% of the retail price for it. It's been this way for thousands of years.

I appreciate the irony that now – close to 14 years later – SCOTTeVEST is finally available through the Hammacher Schlemmer catalog.

I started to learn about e-commerce. I jumped through every hoop needed to set up a credit card processor, merchant account, and shipping accounts. In short order, I became an expert, because I had to become one.

Remember, this is very early 2001, a decade before Kickstarter and Indiegogo. There were no crowdfunding platforms or anything even close to that. The vests were being delivered in a few months and I needed people to buy them now.

It wasn't without glitches, but this was the birth of the pre-order. The sales cycle of apparel was so long that I could go out of business in between shipments if I didn't do pre-orders.

First website, 2001

Roadblocks suck, but they can usually lead you to a better solution.

Cashing In

I didn't exactly realize it at the time, but SCOTTeVEST was the first clothing company launched online. (Okay, okay, we were the first online clothing company that is still in business… I'm looking at you, Zoza, which was founded by the couple behind Banana

Republic). We were started for many, many times less money, too.

In those early days of financial uncertainty, yeah I wanted to get other funding. I would have loved for a VC to sweep in and make me an offer to back my unproven idea. At the time, I would have listened to my *Shark Tank* (rival? arch-enemy? catalyst?) Mark Cuban and gotten investors. But I'm glad I didn't.

The truth is, I was too busy to look for an investor. I looked at how much cash I had in my bank account, then looked harder, calculated what I could live on, used credit cards and took a home equity line of credit (HELOC). I was going to get a small business loan, but it was secured by my house anyway, and the rates were better on the HELOC. I would have sold my car - my primary means of "going fast" - if I had to. I had enough money to get started, but the risk was all mine. It was a comparable risk to the heart, soul, mind and future that I had already bet. I was all in, but that didn't mean I was just going to sit around and wait until July.

If you can't finance your whole business out of your own pockets, look to your potential customers before looking for investors.

I turned to my audience and started pre-selling vests to anyone who wanted one. My main problem was getting more people to know about them.

During SCOTTeVEST's first year of operation, Barry Moltz gave me some of the best advice I have ever received. He is an author and speaker on small businesses and entrepreneurship, and he helped me by looking into my books and telling me what I needed and didn't need. Case in point: I didn't need an investor. My pre-order model could work.

To become successful with this pre-order mechanism, what I really needed was a promoter.

A passionate promoter.

I didn't realize it at the time and I **couldn't** realize it at the time, but everything I had worked for my whole life was coming down to me being right there, right then. This was the moment the real me was born. I just didn't know it yet.

CHAPTER 2
The Birth of a Passionate, Personal Promoter

Anyone can promote himself. Anyone can hire a PR firm, cobble together a press release, and get someone to cover it. The results will be better than if you did nothing, but probably not worth the effort in the long run if that is as far as you go.

For most people, there's an ingredient missing. It's not money or time or writing skills or press contacts. Even utter, soul-sucking desperation is not enough.

If you want to be an effective promoter and achieve a massive level of exposure in the press without paying for it, the main thing you need is absolutely free.

Passion is the foundation of shameless personal promotion.

You could be afraid of public speaking or cold calling, but if you have passion, you'll do them anyway if necessary. You'll do anything you need to do, endure any rejection, hear no 99 times to every single yes. I use the word "shameless" very deliberately, because if you have passion at your core, there is no shame in putting yourself "out there" to show that passion to the world.

If you're hiring someone, hire for passion. You'll know it when you see it. They'll be excited when they win, disappointed when they fail. Passion goes beyond self-interest, and people can sense that, too.

You can't fake passion. It's infectious, and if you're out there promoting yourself, you set the ceiling on passion in every interaction. You need to bring the energy, the passion and excitement to every meeting, every interview, every conversation. No one else can be more passionate about your product or company than you are.

Personal promotion is expressing your passion with a purpose.

I have always been passionate about SCOTTeVEST, even on day one, even when I thought we'd be 90% a licensing company and sell some vests on the side. But I didn't realize how vital my passion was until I put that passion for my brand to the test. Even more important than feeling it is knowing how to communicate it, in person, on the phone, through words and especially in video. Passion is the good side of obsession.

Passion combined with desperation is a powerful recipe for success (if mixed in proper proportions).

This passion is the foundation and driving force for ALL the success I've achieved, even - and especially - right at the beginning. If you start a business wondering how you're going to exit, you probably don't have the passion to sustain it long term anyway.

No Crawling, Just Running

Like the tell-tale heart, I could hear and feel the clock ticking. Every second, every minute, every hour brought me closer to the delivery of the 3,000 vests I ordered and paid for. I was not comforted by the fact that I had a few months to promote them; I was panicked by it. But having the mechanism to pre-sell the items was a necessary step that opened up my opportunities to not just find an audience, but generate money.

In my naiveté, I hired a local Chicago PR firm to help me go after press. They were way over their head when I told them we had to go after major, national media. All they had were excuses. They were used to marketing brands from Chicago in Chicago to Chicago. Maybe a little bit in Wisconsin, too. If I was going to sell thousands of vests, or even hundreds, we needed national exposure. ASAP.

The relationship didn't last long. It was a pattern to be repeated with many PR firms into the future. I want to believe that someone else can promote my brand better than I can, but at the end of the day, passion may be infectious, but being able to communicate it to others may not be.

A Magical Place

I never do just one thing.

If I go to attend a trade show, I sponsor a fan event that night. If I travel to a city, I meet with potential resellers. If I plan a dinner with friends, I try to introduce them to other friends that might be interesting for them to know.

So when the opportunity arose around March of 2001 to go to a mobile computing conference in Orlando, I tallied up all the birds I could kill with that stone.

- Disney vacation for Laura and me. We had already been there a couple times together - seemed like just about every time I changed jobs - and it was always fun.

- The show. It was small - about 250 attendees - but it was mostly full of press folks, and it was at a decent Orlando hotel. Seemed like a pretty good place to meet influential techie people and enterprise level users, and attend a couple lectures.

- My dad. He had remarried within a year of my mom's death to "the woman of his dreams" and was now living in West Palm off the money from the family business he sold out from under me. It sounds crazy, but I was still craving some kind of approval from him. I hadn't spoken to him since I got married, other than when he told my sisters and me that he would write us out of his will if we didn't start getting along after our mom died. I called his bluff, but later it turned out to be true after all. Well, true in my case.

The trip turned out to be my first win on so many levels, and it really got my head "back in the game." Laura and I beat my dad in doubles tennis at the Mar-a-Lago Trump Club tennis courts.

61

She did most of the work on that, which made me love her even more. It might sound petty, but it was a super big deal to me at the time. My dad was a hyper-competitive tennis whiz, and all he did since retirement was play bridge and tennis. So chalk one up for my team.

I was with my dad when I got a call from Dale Coffing of Pocket PC Passion for my largest single pre-order of vests to date. It was a relationship I had been building in the few weeks since I had sent Dale a press release, and he wrote about it on his site. When we first connected, I didn't even realize how influential Dale was, but he soon showed me. After covering SCOTTeVEST the first time, I saw the traffic he generated and sent him a sample vest to check out, then he covered it again. Now, he was placing an order, and my dad was there to witness it.

Dale is a pretty fascinating guy. He's a preacher and started his site because he was passionate about gadgets, not to make money. His enthusiasm inspired me to communicate my own passion, and to seek out people who had the same interests and enthusiasm. Back then, he would drive proportionately more traffic to SeV than most other sites, even today. As great as the exposure was, the sales were what I had to wave in front of my dad. Perfect timing.

It wasn't all roses hanging out in God's waiting room... I mean, the resort community... where my dad lived. As he introduced me around to some of his friends, the common response was that they never knew he had a son. Ouch. No photos of me in his house, either.

I really wanted this trip to be the basis for some sort of a relationship with my dad. I even wanted to get him to invest in my company. It wasn't about the money at all... I really wanted him to be invested in me in some way. Out of the 50/50 split of people who "got it," he was solidly in the non-believing half.

Whatever. We still won in tennis.

It's Showtime

I saw no one I recognized - or had even heard of - at the conference. At the time, I was blanketing anyone who covered any kind of gadgets with press releases, emails, calls and follow-ups. The Compaq iPaq was a pretty hot gadget at the time, and so-called Pocket PCs had a lot of buzz. I had vests designed with tons of pockets. This was a great match.

The more media people I spoke with, the more I recognized that my highest and best use is to talk to the media. It was the first time I realized it, but it's something that I have come back to time and again. It's the core of being a passionate promoter.

The highlight of being at the tradeshow was meeting some reporters, which resulted in one of my favorite articles of all time, titled "Beam Me Up, SCOTTeVEST." They got it, they really got it. After meeting on the event floor, we went up to their hotel room and I did a full demo of the vest. They were my audience, and they were speaking to my audience. Beyond that, they were my first major press article.

It led to more pre-orders for the vest, but I really thought it would open some doors for licensing deals for the patent-pending PAN. There were lots of ebbs and flows in the pre-orders. I sold 200 pretty quickly, but that was a short-lived victory, since it was a drop in the bucket of 3000.

I kept making contacts, sending emails and sending samples, but I needed to make a bigger splash. I was just getting warmed up.

What Fresh Hell Is This? Oh, It's New York.

If you haven't been to New York in July, you have absolutely no idea how blisteringly, brain-fryingly hot it can be. It's not just because of the sun beating down on you, and it's not because NYC can be a pretty intimidating city. It's because of the humidity and the heat bouncing up from the sidewalk after it rains down from above.

In other words, it cooks you from both ends. It was a good thing I was really, really motivated to be there, because if you don't have a great reason to be in NYC in July, there's no reason to be there.

It was 2001, and it was my first time in NYC. I wound up calling Barry Friedland, one of my contractors from New York, every time I got out of a cab or had to cross the street. It was a dizzying experience, and the weather was not cooperating.

It was also the first time I'd worn my eVEST 1.0 in this kind of weather. I wondered if there was anything I could do about how incredibly hot and uncomfortable the eVEST was before the 3,000 unit production run arrived in the next few weeks.

The eVEST 1.0 was a thing of beauty, even though it was non-wicking, all cotton, black and full of 15 pounds of battery-operated shit. 19 pockets carrying my life. Motorola StarTac phone, extra phone batteries, Nikon Coolpix camera, extra camera batteries, Sony Discman, headphones, tons of cords and connectors, wallet, Palm Pilot, spare CF card, CDs and Energizer batteries. Business cards. Tons of business cards... after all, that was why I was here. The Men's Designer Collective was to be my first public trade show demonstrating the eVEST 1.0, and I was here to make an impression.

In terms of style, the eVEST 1.0 was definitely more on the utility end of things. Having said that, no one else seemed to have noticed it was not haute couture, including the costume designers who put it on Matthew McConaughey in the movie *Sahara*.

My experience in NYC started off strong. I was out in the world to pre-sell my vest (at www.scottevest.com - that's Scott like the name, e as in electronics, vest like a vest you wear dot com!). It started on the plane, and I made an impression on the guy in the seat next to me. He said he'd get one when they came out, and I very quickly told him he didn't need to wait... he could pre-order right now. Well, as soon as we landed. We exchanged business cards. I didn't jump up and down in the aisle, but I felt like I just joined the Mile High Club. Figuratively, of course.

I had to make an impression at the show - this show that turned out to be a lot more "fashion" oriented than I even expected - and I was willing to go to any length to do it. I should have realized how fashiony it would be by the name alone, but I was all-in. I set myself up to be a one man promotion machine because I didn't have a booth at the event. My success or failure depended on me and me alone, and the clothes on my back. I was up to the challenge.

I had to make an impression with the reporters and editors my PR firm set up for me to meet in the days after the show. I had hired them to fill the next two days of my trip with back-to-back press interviews, and they told me I would be thrilled with the interviews they lined up for me. I had to put my best foot forward, and as I melted into a sweaty mess, I didn't feel like I was off to a good start.

Sitting in the back of the crosstown cab that reeked of stale curry and cheap cologne attempting to mask the driver's body odor, the hot air was blowing in through the open windows when we were moving, and sitting thick and still when we weren't. I had my elevator pitch worked out to the point that it was boring to go over it any more. I even literally pitched the elevator operator at the hotel, and to this day, it tickles me to give elevator pitches in elevators and to talk to people wearing other brands of vests. I'm sure some people think I'm crazy.

I pitched the cabbie, and I think I got through to him. I knew the show was being held at one of the pier buildings on the Hudson River, so we were getting close.

Maybe the heads/tails 50/50 rule was shifting in my favor.

I took a deep breath and raised my passionate personal promotion level to DEFCON 8, and every light, siren and alarm in my mind was ready to make this trip work. It was like standing on the edge of a cliff and leaping without looking. Failure was not an option.

It's Showtime (Again)

My decision not to get a $4K booth was based on my confidence that I could just walk around, press the flesh and show off my vest to anyone and everyone in the crowd that would listen. The press covered trade shows like this, so if I hung out by the press room, I was bound to meet the right people. I asked my PR firm to set up some meetings at the show, but nothing came of it. I was on my own.

I knew they would want to hear what I had to say... they were all fashion people, right? Surely they would be riveted by the most interesting thing that's been done with pockets since... well, the invention of pockets. This was tech-enabled clothing, and I invented it. As much as I was looking for pre-orders of the vest, I knew that licensing my patent (pending) Personal Area Network (PAN) was going to be my biggest play, and getting major press coverage was the way to do both.

"Hi, I'm Scott Jordan and --"

Wow, so that's what the evil eye looks like.

These weren't gadget people. These weren't techies. They were dyed in the wool fashionistas and they could not care less about speaking to me. I homed in on a few meek looking booth helpers and gave them my licensing pitch, but it was fruitless.

If you've ever been to a show at the piers in NYC, you know they're just cavernous warehouse spaces, and while you might not get lost there, you also might not know where you need to go. I wandered around for three hours, talking to people - anyone who would listen - and showing off my proudest achievement, the vest. My cheeks hurt from smiling. My voice was getting hoarse from speaking over the din of the crowd. And I was getting more frustrated and pissed with each quarter-interested interaction.

I didn't expect to close any licensing deals on the spot, but I also didn't feel like I was selling the idea of it either. My 50/50 rule fell flat, and I didn't even get to meet any press at the show. I just looked like a flasher showing off my pockets.

If there was one bright spot, it was meeting Clinton Kelly, a fashion reporter and TV host who eventually did cover SCOTTeVEST a few times over the years. He's a co-host on The Chew now, and he "got" what I was doing with the company. At least one person did.

By early afternoon, I was hot and my vest was pulling down on my neck and giving me a headache. When I finally found the gray, concrete bunker-styled men's room and saw myself in the mirror, I looked like a sweaty, red, disheveled mess.

"Fuck it, I'm going back to the hotel."

As I wound my way through the rows of booths and out to the blinding light of the street, my headache got even worse. I speed walked toward the doors, and it was even hotter than when I arrived in the morning. Looking down the street, there were no cabs in sight, and the line at the taxi stand was thirty people deep.

I walked, all the way back to the hotel, and I doubted myself for the first time since I started SCOTTeVEST.

Round Two

I let the door slam behind me. They were fired. They would get paid, but they would be gone just as soon as I got back to Chicago.

They weren't the first PR firm I fired, and they would prove to not be the last, either. I couldn't believe that they were recommended to me.

While walking to the hotel from the convention center, somewhere between 39th and 40th street, I stopped feeling sorry for myself, and decided that if the convention was going to be a bust, I needed to start my press tour a day early. The PR firm was able to move up our kickoff meeting, and that change was what I needed to get myself back on track.

As you can tell by the slamming door, it didn't exactly work. I expected to receive an agenda from my expert PR firm with meeting after meeting with press lined up for the next two days. I counted on not being able to eat because I was so busy. I practiced apologies for being late because my *Today Show* interview went long.

They booked me for a grand total of three interviews in two days, and they expected me to not only do backflips, but to throw money - a lot more money - at them. I could do three interviews in an hour. I've set up three interviews in an hour. This was not a victory; this was not worth my trip to New York.

These twenty-something PR "experts" told me that no one "got" the vest, and they'd be better off pitching it once we had some big sales figures behind us. It was a comment I heard from many other PR firms over the years.

How am I supposed to get sales without press??? My mind calculated the costs... two thousand dollars for them, the plane ticket, a hotel room, a blood pressure spike, three days of my time, meals, cabs.... The bottom line? PR firms are useless.

I've paid big firms like MSLGROUP to create press kits and book a presentation for me at the MAGIC conference (not magical, it's clothing related). There wasn't a single person in the audience.

I've had such junior people assigned to my account that they didn't follow up with samples, their grammar was atrocious and because I was never CCd on communications, I wasn't even sure they did any outreach.

It's counter-intuitive... there are so many huge firms. Every so often, I think I'm wrong and I hire one, and every single time it doesn't work out. Maybe there is just a larger margin or tolerance for failure at bigger corporations. I want to believe someone else can do PR for me, but I have never seen it happen. I've been through at least 12 PR firms.

If you want PR, you need to go out and get it yourself.

I was on fire, and almost literally. I had two days, and I was going to prove them wrong. I was going to do what they couldn't. I was going to make it look easy.

I was not going home empty handed.

Hitting the Hot Pavement

It was 90 degrees by 8AM, I was full of coffee and I was in the fight of my life.

My scheduled interviews went well, and I was able to channel all my determination into delivering passionate but clear interviews.

In retrospect, they were pretty solid opportunities, but my main problem was that there weren't nearly enough of them. In 2001, print magazines were still actually printed, and most of them were monthlies. Any coverage I got could be a few months out, and maybe that would be a few months too late. Any newspaper coverage could be immediate, but it also disappeared immediately.

I had to get more, and I was going to walk around until I found out how much "more" I could get. Maps? We don't need no stinking maps. If there was a press outlet worthy of speaking to, their name would be on the building. Oh, and it would be a BIG building. Why would I want to talk to anyone less than the best?

I was on foot and walking as fast as the most jaded New Yorkers. *The New York Times*, ABC, NBC. My approach: walk in, put on my most sincere looking smile and ask the receptionist to direct me to the floor where anyone who covers clothing, technology or travel works.

What?

"I'm the CEO of a clothing company that makes vests for carrying..."

If I didn't have an appointment, of course I couldn't get in. I couldn't even get the names of anyone who worked there. I knew that if I was given a chance - just one chance - to speak to a reporter or editor that my passion would shine through and they'd love my product.

At least one of the receptionists thought I was a little crazy. I don't really have a filter or a dial when I'm presenting my products to someone. If I start a pitch, the fire hose is fully open every time. I pulled out all the stops, and came across with the same level of passion speaking to the person behind the reception desk as I would to the editor of *The New York Times*. Most of the receptionists loved it, and if it was up to them, they would not only have let me in, but put me on the front cover, too.

The problem was that my message was lost in translation. They just couldn't convey my passion well enough when they called upstairs, and no one took the bait. Although they were the all-important first gatekeeper, they didn't have the clout to get me through.

I left lobby after lobby with pockets full of gadgets, wires sticking out of my collar and sweat running down my back.

Conde Nast, *New York Post*, CBS, *Wall Street Journal*, *The New York Times*. It seemed like the 50% non-believers turned into 90%. I continued, mostly undeterred. Someone WILL speak to me. With each rejection, each denial I become more determined. More determined to prove the PR folks wrong. More determined to prove the non-believing 50% of people I've told about SCOTTeVEST wrong. More determined that today was going to be the day that put SeV on the map in the national media.

The Cold Lobby

It was getting late in the afternoon, and while my brain was willing, my body needed some A/C. I saw the Time-Life building... I've heard of *TIME Magazine*, who hasn't? Perfect target.

The Time-Life lobby was freezing - which was exactly what I needed. As much as I wanted to collect myself on the couch, the lobby was small enough that I couldn't ignore the receptionist.

"I'm here to see the editor."

She smiled, looked behind her at the lit up directory of floors, then turned her amused gaze slowly back at me. "Which one?" she asked.

I strained to see the sign and realized that Time-Life wasn't just *TIME Magazine*, but dozens of publications... and they were all in this building. Jackpot?

"All of them." I didn't hesitate, I didn't waver. She didn't stop smiling, but she also didn't move.

"I'm the CEO of a clothing company that makes vests for carrying..."

"Hold on, hold on," she interrupted as I pulled my phone, some batteries and a pack of gum from my pockets and hurriedly plopped them on her counter.

"You don't need to convince me. You need to convince them," she continued, motioning to the directory. "Which editors do you want to talk to?"

"Technology... fashion... travel... and pop culture."

She slid a clipboard across the counter to me. It was a call sheet with thousands of names and numbers for the reporters and editors I wanted to see. When I read what it was, I looked up at her, then back at the paper.

"If you can get someone to talk to you, I'll send you up."

I could sit in the lobby - the beautifully frosty, cool lobby - and call everyone in the building? Win-win. I would be heading upstairs in five minutes, and I'd even have a chance to cool off.

The As: Voicemail. Voicemail.

The Bs: Voicemail. Voicemail. Voicemail.

The Cs....

I realized that many would probably be screening their calls, so I left a message at the beep. At every beep. I talked fast through every part of every message, except my phone number, which I repeated twice. By the time I reached the single Z name, I'm sure the receptionist regretted giving me the list. I left dozens of messages.

No missed calls on my cell. No ringing phone in my hand. I didn't even get through to one live person out of at least forty. Nothing. I was going home with nothing. All of a sudden, the air conditioning started to feel too cold.

I thanked her as I returned the list and left the lobby. I was going home. Not just to the hotel, but home. I waved down a cab and called Laura to have her look up when the next flight from JFK to Chicago was. PR firm: 1. Me: zero. New York: 1. Me: zero.

I was pissed and disappointed and cold and hot and confused. I didn't know where things stood. I didn't care if I had to sit in the airport for six hours. It was the first – and last – time I ever quit.

A Short Ride

I closed my eyes in the back of the cab to JFK.

Then I felt it... the vibration of my phone in my perfectly designed pocket, working exactly the way I designed it to work. At least the vest worked correctly. I fumbled the phone from my pocket in a way I hadn't done the other eighty times I took it out today. It was a 212 number.

"Hi, may I speak to Scott Jordan? This is Jodi from *TIME Magazine.* You left me a message..."

I won after all.

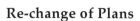

Re-change of Plans

Just as quickly as the cab could turn around, I went back to the Time-Life lobby. I only had about 15 minutes to collect my thoughts and air out the vest in the breeze of the open taxi window. It was the best I could do to dry out my SWEAT-eVest to make sure it looked and smelled as fresh as possible for the occasion. I called Laura back to tell her what was happening, and although she played it cool (as she always does), I knew she was excited for me.

The same receptionist was there, and she gave me a strange look while she tried to figure out if I got a call back or if I was going to be a problem.

"Hi - I have an appointment with Jodi at *TIME*." She smiled at me while she called up to confirm, and then directed me to the right elevator.

"Good for you," she said and smiled ear to ear. I could tell that she was rooting for me, and felt partially responsible for helping me reach my goal. I learned something from that smile: bring people along for the ride. If you care about what you're doing - really care - and communicate that, many people will want you to succeed. For every internet troll, there is a hopeful supporter.

The rest, as they say, is history.

The History of the Rest

Ok, so the rest was not quite so historic. We had a great conversation and talked for the better part of an hour. We became best friends. I went off-script and my passion came through like never before. There was no tension, and she told me that she would write about me in the next issue. Guaranteed. In fact, she was on deadline and my article would come out the next week (this was back when *TIME Magazine* killed trees four times a month rather than killing pixels). She loved the vest and everything it stood for, and I gave her the eVEST 1.0 off my back for her to keep.

She gave me the plastic Fairway bag from her lunch to carry all my gadgets home. I was thrilled to hand over my sample, but it honestly was really inconvenient for me to get back home... like before I invented the SCOTTeVEST. It was the only sample I had, and I wondered what would happen if I didn't get it back. There were bigger concerns at the time, though.

My head was spinning on the flight home to Chicago. List... I needed to make a list.

- Set up a phone bank
- Find a staffing firm to man the phone bank
- Make sure the site won't crash from the *TIME* traffic
- Find the latest date I could increase my order with the factory without causing delays
- Send the clipping from *TIME* to the PR firm after it runs and get in the last word
- ...and about three dozen other items

It would be a crazy week of late nights and early mornings to get ready for the magazine to drop, but it would be worth it. I wasn't coming home empty handed. I was coming home with *TIME Magazine.*

The day the new issue came out, I was torn. Can I spare the time away from the phone and computer to run out and pick up a copy? I did. I leafed through the issue at the newsstand before paying for it. Cover to cover. Nothing.

Did Jodi have the wrong dates? Was this the wrong issue? I had just gotten an email from her yesterday, so it should be here. I flipped through again, and then I saw it...

IN BRIEF

Earphones

Wireless Phone

Digital Organizer

Laptop (inside)

STYLE FILE Belt clips aren't the only way for geeks to carry their gear. The Scott eVest ($160), made of a water-repellent, cotton-blend fabric, conceals a dozen pockets that are designed for everything from laptops to PDAs. Velcro tabs along the edges hold wires in place, and an opening near the neckline keeps your cell phone's earpiece handy. The eVest comes in black and khaki. A version for women is on the way.

Circa August 2001

What? That's it? No website, no phone number? No mention of the revolutionary personal area network?

Two orders. Two orders from *TIME Magazine*. I'm sure they could hear me yelling all the way from Chicago.

Post Mortem

At this point, I had learned a bunch of things:

- I should do my own PR.
- Seeing reporters in person is overrated and unnecessary. Email and phone should suffice for much of it.
- Getting an article without a URL or at least a phone number mentioned in it is useless.
- There is no magic bullet, no matter how big the publication.

I also learned that my shipment of vests had left China, and would be arriving in the US in about four weeks. As exciting as that was, and although I had pre-sold several hundred by this point, I hadn't **pre-sold nearly enough of them** and had to keep the momentum going. Beyond putting my scheduling in the hands of people who didn't "get" my product, what could I do better to ensure that all the rest of the press would have maximum impact? What did I do that worked?

Control the Message

I sent a lot of press releases. I sent press releases about the eVEST 1.0 when it was developed, when it was ordered and when it shipped. I wrote about the Personal Area Network. I would scour through Google for links to people, forums, and blogs that needed to know about it, and it was through doing this that I got my first real exposure, even before my trip to New York.

I also developed some KILLER press kits early in the SCOTTeVEST era. Usually, they were laminated and had multiple sheets with a personal note, a press release, information about our products, our story and graphics explaining how everything worked. It was the first version of the "pocket map" we still use today to show all the pockets and hidden features in our vests and jackets. To show off the Personal Area Network, every sample was wired with headphones, and no sample ever left my hands without a 20 page press kit going with it. The press kit included directions, a company history, contact information, where to download images, my bio and tons of company press clippings.

I wondered if there was a secret to which press releases were picked up, and which ones fall flat. There is. I hate things like "Scott's 10 Rules for Press Releases," so you'll need to imagine these as numbered if that's what floats your boat.

- Most reporters are some combination of lazy and busy. The more your story is served to them on a silver cut-and-paste platter, the more likely they are to run it. If you make their jobs easier, they'll publish your stuff time and again.

- If you screw up the basics, you've completely wasted your time, even if you get press on the front page of the *Wall Street Journal*. The basics are...

  o Provide a cut-and-paste-able press release.

  o Include your company name, URL and/or phone number in ways that are impossible to cut out.

  o Don't just embed a link to your site, spell it out: www.scottevest.com. When embedded links get pasted into some blog editors, the link is lost unless the URL is in the text.

  o Provide easy access to images (high-res) with a clear link to where to download them. Be ready to get them assets in their preferred format if they have a special request. It's not hard.

  o Be available to questions within five minutes of receiving them. Speed is essential. If they want to talk to you, don't wait.

  o Have samples ready to send, but don't just send them out to everyone. Be selective (more on that later).

- It's NOT bad to write a press release as if it were a marketing piece. It is. Unless you're pitching to an academic trade journal, the tone can be pretty casual. Toot your horn. Remember... they're probably going to just paste it, so what do you want them to say? In actuality, you're writing an article, not a press release.

- Craft your own sound bytes. Here are some of my favorite quotes about me and SCOTTeVEST:

  o "Imagine Bill Gates and Giorgio Armani stranded alone on a desert island, and you'll have a good idea of what the SCOTTeVEST TEC Sport Jacket offers."

  o "SCOTTeVEST is the most significant thing to happen to clothing since the bikini."

Do you know what these very complimentary quotes have in common? I said them, and they were quoted in publications. In fact, the Bill Gates quote was used by *Fortune* Magazine. Now and until the end of time, I can repeat them and attribute them to these fine media outlets. All because I gave them what I wanted them to say, and they said it. We were one of *USA Today's* Top Tech Gifts in 2001, but that quote is still just as true today.

You Can't Control the Message

It's a problem. You need to control the message, but ultimately, it's up to the publication... the writer, the editor, the publisher... someone other than you. As much as I learned and as finely crafted my press releases and contacts were in theory, you will (almost) never get a chance to comment and make edits before an article goes live.

It's happened again and again and again.

SCOTTeVEST has been featured on *The Today Show* maybe 3 or 4 times since starting the company. If you told me on Day 1 that I could say this someday, I would have assumed I would have a hundred million dollars in the bank. Ummm, I don't. So why not?

The first four times the product was shown - yes FOUR, as in the number of letters in all the words I said after the shows aired - they failed to mention the company name, URL or both. Four appearances, no mention. You can see a video of one of those times here, and hear me yelling at the TV∗. I did everything right. I followed my own rules, provided quick feedback, sent samples, blah blah blah. I couldn't make the hosts say the words on live TV. It wasn't a snub, just an oversight.

I've done custom photoshoots, written a page of great material and had graphic designers spend hours creating amazing images to wind up with a blurb and no URL printed (I'm looking at you, *NY Times*).

∗ www.scottevest.com/todayshowfail

78

But You Need to Control the Message Anyway

Whether an opportunity fell far flat of my expectations or not, I always took control of the message. If a magazine didn't publish enough details to bring customers to my site, I still told everyone I knew about the exposure. There's power in being featured in a publication even if you don't get any immediate, direct sales from it.

Similar principles hold true with product placement. We've been featured in a dozen episodes of NBC's CHUCK, ABC's Flash Forward, HBO's The Wire, Matthew McConaughey wore SeV in Sahara, Steve Martin wore us in The Big Year, and on and on. No one sees the label on the clothes, no one does the research, barely any searches, no sales. But I can - and do - say that we've been featured in all these places. When we were on CHUCK, we sent a press release. Product placement is only as valuable as you make it.*

Books are a somewhat different story, since a lot of readers are willing to do the research, and the company or product name is there in black and white. Ridley Pearson has included us in several of his books, as has Brad Thor and several other authors. We've even been featured in several textbooks. Exposure is either a division game or a multiplication game. You can either rely on a fraction of the readership to do the research and find you (division), or you can promote the fact that you were in a book to everyone (multiplication). Associating with these authors and books can translate to real money, but don't expect a summer home from the deal.

Won an award? Same approach. We've been in INC.'s Fastest Growing Companies list for many years, Internet Retailer's Hot 100, the IR Mobile 500, Apparel Magazine's most innovative companies, were featured in The New York Times Magazine's Year in Ideas issue and won other awards I can't even remember. All an award does is give you something to talk about. Use it as an opportunity to do so, and you'll be getting the best thing you can from them. If you don't use it as an opportunity, all you'll be left

---

* You can see a sizzle reel at www.scottevest.com/sizzle

79

with are the dozens of sales pitches you receive once the winners list has been published.

One More Thing

If you're not using video now, you're missing out. If you're not comfortable using video, work on it. It's the closest thing you can get to face-to-face interaction with people without going on a tour, setting dozens of meetings, and taking on all the expenses associated with it. Even if you prefer meeting in person, you can't deny that video has a vastly better Return on Investment (ROI).

Video is the ultimate tool for controlling the message and communicating your passion.

While creative editing (more on that in the *Shark Tank* section of the book) can twist and change messages, you still have more control over the message when you use video than anything else.

Don't worry about spending a lot of money on a fancy setup. We took over a room in our office and converted it into a video studio with lights, teleprompter and a full wall greenscreen setup. We spent significant time and money, only to discover that the camera settings we had been using for over a year were wrong. All that work to screw up on a basic thing?

That's when we went back to unscripted videos, and I shoot most of them with the camera on my computer or with my iPhone. Unscripted videos are easy, and they let your personality come through. They definitely get easier the more you do it, and it's not intimidating like speaking in front of a crowd can be.

Just about every day, I send three off the cuff video emails. Depending on the circumstances, I'll either use MailVU or record the video directly into YouTube and share it as "unlisted." They are personal messages from me (one person) to someone else (another one person). This makes for a powerful one on one connection, and by, you know, saying their name, they know this is a message just for them. I've taken time from my life to connect with them, and only them.

A lot of people believe they know me personally because I have done this, and for the most part, they're right whether they are customers, reporters, or interviewees. Communicating passion is huge, and I haven't found a better or faster way to do it than through video. How else can you make such as strong connection in six minutes a day with three people that you may or may not know?

I've even had some vendors ask if they can use videos I've sent them publicly, or if I can shoot an endorsement specifically for them. HQTS is my factory inspection team, and they visited my office in Idaho in part to get a video with me for promotion purposes. Same thing with the A/B testing provider Frictionless Commerce. Miva is our long-time shopping cart platform, and they even sent a professional film crew to get my video endorsement. Passionate promoter tip: they all spent their time and money to develop and promote me talking about them. Free exposure, easy setup... all because of video.

Using video this way has even been the start of some great working relationships and friendships. Years ago, we received an order from someone named Amy Tan. My wife Laura was a fan of her books - well, the books of the author Amy Tan, at least - so we decided to reach out to her and ask if she was "the" Amy Tan. She was.

We replied with a quick, simple, but personal email to let her know how much we enjoyed her work, and appreciated her business. We continued to communicate, and have built a friendship over time, visiting each other when we can.

CHAPTER 3
Easy Opportunities

One thing I learned immediately after forming SCOTTeVEST: everyone thinks they have nothing to talk about. That one misguided belief is what has held back every company that falls short on promotion, and I was not going to fall into that trap. I always have something to discuss, promote and share - even if it hasn't happened yet, or even if it happened years ago - you can repurpose anything.

I've (re-)started conversations by "liking" something on Facebook from four years ago. If you are doing anything even mildly interesting - and you're doing it with passion - you have something to promote.

I have plenty of stories, and while this chapter may seem to be filled with many "small" stories, it's the sum total that has made SCOTTeVEST successful. A lot of personal promotion is not hard, but it requires persistence and passion.

If you don't believe in yourself, your company or your product enough to "get out there," then just roll over right now. There's no point in trying to promote something you're not passionate about, because your lack of fire will put out any potential caring that someone else could experience. Do yourself a favor and just quit.

But....

If you're willing to put yourself on the line like I did, and continue to do, and you are inspired by what I've done, this is how I built the foundation of my personally-promoted pocket empire.

Let's Give Them Something to Talk About

Here's the thing. If you don't have something even mildly interesting to talk about, no one in the press (even bloggers) will cover your story. It doesn't need to change the world, and the bar for "mildly interesting" can be set pretty low, but there needs to at least be a hook. Even if it's not interesting to anyone at face value, it's your job to make it sound like it is.

The word "new" is one of the ultimate - and most overused - hooks, and that's why product launches are the cornerstone of personal promotion. It doesn't matter if the product is a vest, a book (*cough*), a new color toothbrush, a limited edition that comes with a free sticker or a new jet. A product launch is a golden opportunity, and I've made more gold from these types of opportunities than just about any other.

Losing My Version-ity: 1.0, 2.0, 3.0

The first SCOTTeVEST was the eVEST 1.0, and if you are even moderately tech-savvy, you know that is a nod to how versions of software are labeled. When we started, I thought it was a clever reference to the gadget and computer world, and it had the added bonus of building in obsolescence. I wanted people to buy a new version of my products each year, if only because there was a new one. It's worked for cars for over 100 years, so why not for my vests?

Because I could market vests the way software companies marketed, there would be an instant understanding with my tech-oriented audience. I could test out features as "betas" and if something didn't work, they just wouldn't appear in the next one. Special editions could be created during production, and the difference might be minor - a black zipper instead of a metal one - but now I had a "Stealth Edition" to sell... and promote. With the right product, versions can be a great way to get press without reinventing the whole wheel each time.

Months after the eVEST 1.0 launch, even before we completely sold through the first 3,000 units, we created a 2.0 version with removable sleeves. Basically, it was the eVEST 1.0 with sleeves, and now it was a jacket. Pre-orders led to orders and I had a whole new version to talk about.

The 3.0 followed, because that's how math works, and we kept improving incrementally. With each new version, we could also test out different types of messaging to see what worked best. Did you know that the eVEST 3.0 Plus had 2,312.75 square inches of pocket capacity (excluding depth)? It didn't matter that the factory could only source black zippers at a good price because we now could call it a "Stealth Version."

Changing anything in a product or its messaging - even if it's minor - is important because it gives you a new hook to talk about.

Versioning worked well for many years and continues to do so. As of fall 2014, we are up to version 8.0 of our Fleece Jacket, although we skipped 6.0 because Laura hates that number. You get to do things like that when you're your own boss.

Dealing with the Vests in Hand

When the first 3,000 eVEST 1.0s arrived in August 2001, I learned a lot of things.

I learned that pre-orders were vital to my success and cash flow, and that all the technical issues we overcame to do them were ultimately worth the headache.

I learned that having a few thousand vests sitting in a warehouse (which was also my office) can really light a fire under my ass and make me promote even harder. And I learned that every bit of promotion that I've done was not enough.

By the time they arrived, we had already been covered by *BusinessWeek*, *Playboy*, *Digital Camera Magazine*, *Handheld*

Computing magazine, *Maximum PC*, and more. *ABC News**
covered us at 3AM, and Laura saw it while on the treadmill and
came running up the stairs calling out to me. How were these
vests not completely sold out?

I had to keep pushing. I emailed bloggers (were they even
called bloggers then?), forum owners, reporters, editors and TV
anchors. I followed up time and again. I found new reasons to
reach out to people who had already covered us, and I got them to
cover us again. This was the start of building relationships with
media people, and this was a huge part of my success as a
promoter. The more fun the interactions were, the better the
coverage, and I treated every media person like gold.

No one would get a sample without a commitment to either
write about the product or to return it. I knew that I could sell
every single vest if I had enough time, so sending a sample and
not getting coverage was a total waste. I recently found an old
handwritten spreadsheet of who I sent samples to, when they
committed to review them, and a list of follow-up dates. I didn't
need a fancy CRM system or a staff of 12 to do it. Just the
determination to know it had to be done if I was going to make
the most of every opportunity.

Feedback

Once the pre-ordered eVEST 1.0s shipped, people started to
review them online. They were amazingly positive. There was
nothing even remotely like this on the market, but still to this day,
I think it was a pretty obvious idea. My feedback went from
50/50 to 100% positive, because only people who "got" the idea
invested in one. They were not disappointed, and I wasn't the
only one to notice.

Unbeknownst to me, my credit card processing company had
a policy of checking up on their new account holders to make sure
they were actually sending out the products their customers paid
for. This was 2001, so e-commerce was not prevalent at all, and
there was a lot of fear of internet fraud.

---

* www.scottevest.com/abcnews

The credit card company would take a random sample of transactions and follow up with the customers by calling them on the phone. When the customers picked up, they were pretty ambiguous about who they represented, and said something to the effect of, "Hi, we're calling to make sure everything is OK with your recent SCOTTeVEST order...."

Naturally, the customers assumed they were talking to someone from SCOTTeVEST.

A few weeks after starting their "investigation" I received a call from the credit card company. They had a big problem.

It turned out that every person they called did assume they were talking to someone from my company, and they gushed and raved about how much they loved the product. The card company couldn't get these people off the phone! Their reps were being given product demos over the phone, listening as the customers rattled off all the stuff they were able to carry, and found out that two out of three people they spoke to were wearing their eVESTs when they picked up the phone.

Our products had not only met their expectations, but exceeded them. This was good because it meant we had a great product, but it has been a consistent struggle for us to show the product on the site well enough to close that expectation gap. I'm convinced that more people would buy up front if they could experience how good the product actually is.

The card processor had never heard of such enthusiastic responses, and they broke protocol to tell me about it. I was a little pissed that they felt the need to follow up with customers, but I was elated by the response. It also reinforced what I had discovered every time I showed someone my invention:

SCOTTeVESTs are very demonstrable.

It wasn't just my "amazing" showmanship, but the fact that people wanted to show theirs off that would help me sell. Doing it in person was one thing, but showing off online would provide a much broader reach. I'll go deeper into how I leveraged customer photos later, but it was really important for me to jump into every online conversation about my products. I would comment on every review, answer every question and make any problem right.

To this day, I fight to have the best Customer Service in the business because nothing cuts the legs out from under your ability to promote faster than shitty CS. Each well-done review is like a demonstration, and gets the audience engaged. A positive experience is amplified, and so is a negative one. That's why CS is so vital. I am as passionate about great Customer Service as I am about promotion.

That doesn't mean the customer is always right. In fact, the customer is only right if they're not wrong. I've never backed down from any internet troll, and we have enforced a Seinfeld "Soup Nazi"-style "no vest for you!" policy.

There is a blacklist of customers to whom we will not sell products, and you will find yourself on that list if you treat our CS team shittily. Laura takes delight in tracking down people who try to circumvent the list by shipping to friends, etc. That's how seriously we take these situations.

I've even emailed "exploding" videos to some people who deserved a piece of my mind. Of course, these videos are automatically removed from the hosting site after they are played once, effectively blowing them up *Mission Impossible* style.

Fortunately, these are pretty extreme situations, and most interactions are incredibly positive. But in any case, if there's a conversation about my products, I'm going to be part of it.

Insert Yourself into the Conversation

Realistically, you probably can't launch a new product each week, unless you are like my friends at Betabrand, who do exactly that. But this is a book about me, not them, so just assume you can't launch a new product every week. That doesn't get you off the hook for personal promotion.

When you can't start a conversation, insert yourself into one. It's a lot easier to be pulled along with momentum than to start from a dead stop. It doesn't even need to be very complicated, but it's an essential mindset.

For years, every time a new product came out, I would visit the links for all the previous articles and reviews about SCOTTeVEST, and post a new comment about it on their page. This applied to blogs, major press, forums… everywhere. Most of the time, if a new comment is posted about an article that someone has commented on or subscribed to, they are emailed when a new comment has been added. Essentially, if someone was interested in a previous topic mentioning SCOTTeVEST, I could very easily make it fresh in their minds by re-commenting about the latest development.

Don't be a total douche when you chime in, but don't try to hide your intentions. The message must be personalized and relevant (which takes time), or you're just a spammer. If you're there to promote your product, don't be shy about it… be shameless. People may not like it, but if your intentions are clear, there will be people who notice. Just don't use the same cut-and-paste message all over the place. Not only is it ineffective, but it's a negative mark on you and your brand.

Doing this one thing must have made me hundreds of thousands of dollars over the years.

Too bad it doesn't work with Twitter. It can kinda be done on Facebook by liking or commenting on old posts.

It even works with news stories that (initially) have nothing to do with your brand. There was an article that came out just this week (when writing) that included a photo of Matthew McConaughey wearing a fanny pack. He had worn a SCOTTeVEST years ago in the film *Sahara*, so this was an opportunity for us to insert ourselves into the public conversation by commenting on it. It's also a potential icebreaker for a public figure or celebrity that is personally involved in their own social media. He wouldn't be the first star to personally reply to a tweet or DM from me.

But how do you know what conversations are happening? First, you need to be out in the world. I consume a ton of media every day...including TV, news, articles, blog posts, and social media. I personally keep my finger on the pulse of what's going on. That drives where I turn my attention.

Google Alerts are a necessary tool. They're free, and basically Google will email you automatically with search results for whatever terms you want. I've found out about more mentions of SCOTTeVEST than I would ever have found on my own because of Google Alerts. Search results for my name, key terms like "fanny packs" (because our pockets make them unnecessary) and brand terms are all delivered to me automatically, as often as there is activity around them.

I'm always ready to pounce on an opportunity. But sometimes, opportunities aren't your biggest concern.

That Tuesday

It was September of 2001, and I still had about 2,000 vests left from the initial 3,000 order. I was making press contacts constantly, and I even reached out to *TIME* again and got them to agree to a "real" article. Things were lining up nicely. NPR scheduled me to appear as a guest, and I knew that would get us to the next level. We were not only getting some traction with the geeky gadget loving early adopters, but travelers began seeing the benefit of a multi-pocket alternative to a carry-on.

The business was picking up speed and then....

It was a dark time for everyone, and a dark time for me. The business could fail. *TIME* had more pressing things to write about. NPR had more pressing things to talk about. The rules of travel changed. The world was a different place. Everyone was afraid of what "they" would do next, and my one and only product was a vest designed to have wires run through it. Great.

Little by little, things returned to a new version of normal, and America as a whole got back to business, but with much higher security concerns. I had to get creative.

Travel was a hot topic, and it became harder for the average person, and definitely more of a hassle. It took some time, but as people took to the air again, they needed a more efficient way to get through security checkpoints. The first few times I traveled, I wondered if airport security would make me empty all my pockets. If that became the norm, my company would be sunk.

But they didn't. And as my customers gave me new feedback about traveling through airports with a SCOTTeVEST, their reports were consistent: you could just take off the vest and put it through the x-ray machine. Years later, I would find out that many TSA agents are actually trained about SCOTTeVESTs. Because you don't need to empty your pockets, we make travel a breeze.

Entrepreneur magazine picked up on this, and featured SCOTTeVEST in an article about ways to make travel easier post 9/11. We were highlighted as an up-and-coming company, and they went on to send out a photographer and profile me a few years later. For someone who had majored in Entrepreneurship, this was the ultimate validation.

With some added financial uncertainty, the $159.99 looked more and more like a barrier to entry. I had to lower it, but I didn't want to look like a schmuck doing it. I just had 1,000 people - my earliest, truest believers - pay full price. I couldn't afford to give them refunds, but I needed a way to get it down to a price point that more people could swallow.

I did that by making them scarce.

Sold Out

The first batch of SCOTTeVESTs were sold out. Or rather, "sold out." The pre-order worked so well, that I put them back on pre-order, and I was bringing this second batch out at a lower price.* I was sitting on a couple thousand perfectly good vests for a month, and it was not my most upfront strategy of all time, but this was a pretty unique situation.

It worked. We were back in business, and with the holiday approaching, I was becoming confident again for the first time in awhile that financial conditions would continue to improve.

---

* See the press release here - www.scottevest.com/soldout

Guilty By Association

While the scarcity model helped to get us back on track, it was a sales strategy, not a promotion strategy. We were still a very small fish in a very big pond. That was really encouraging because it meant we had plenty of potential to grow.

All of the gadgets and devices that the eVEST 1.0 could carry were from huge, well established brands. I didn't need to look farther than my own pockets to find some powerful coattails to ride. People's minds are designed to pick up on details and specificity. You can gloss over a watch, but a Rolex Submariner catches your attention, and says something about the person wearing it.

We took photos of models wearing SeV and a Rolex. We took photos of someone wearing their eVEST and the famous Adidas striped track pants. I was even in some photos wearing my eVEST and a Xybernaut eyepiece, which was the Google Glass of its day. These were the kinds of brands that our customers knew and loved - or in some cases aspired to have - and we portrayed our product on par with them.

Circa March 2002

In the same way, what you carried in your SCOTTeVEST pockets said something about you, and since I was painting the picture of the SeV customer, I was going to make sure the eVEST was depicted with the hottest of the hot brands and their latest devices:

- You wouldn't just carry a phone in your eVEST, you would carry a Motorola StarTAC.
- It wasn't a music device, it was a SONY Discman.
- That's no generic PDA, it's a Compaq iPaq.
- And starting in October of 2001, it became all about the Apple iPod.

94

That pocket-sized music device with iconic white earbuds was the embodiment of what this vest was designed to carry. People who "got" the iPod, got SCOTTeVEST, too. To this day, a huge percentage of our website visitors come to us on an Apple device, and I've been flattered to be referred to many times as "the Steve Jobs of clothing."

The iPod was a gadget-lover's gadget, and I had already designed the ultimate iPod accessory. It even said so on my website, so you know it must have been true.

More recently, Guy Kawasaki said, "Wow, there's more design thought in these garments than most smart phones." That idea has been part of our design philosophy since before there were smart phones. It's amazing how compatible the thinking can be between two very different, but interconnected industries.

Every graphic, every photo, every interview, every recording, every video, every press release reinforced the connection that these brands were in good company with SCOTTeVEST. I still do this today, and our ten foot wide tradeshow booth shows larger than life graphics of real devices from real brands. We have never said that any of these great brands have endorsed us, and there have never been any objections.

We've even issued press releases when big corporations like Intel and Microsoft place an order for products for their employees. It's never been a problem, but I'd rather seek forgiveness than ask permission. The iron has plenty of time to cool off while waiting for a go-ahead, and it's always important to strike while it's hot.

Any bit of association you can make with an established brand will help you get more attention.

Have Fun

One of the best things about the iPod, and Apple's marketing in general, is that it was never just about what you were buying, but why. Their "Think Different" campaign was amazing, and the early iPod ads made the products seem like they were fun to own. I loved their products, loved their attitude and advertising, but lacked their budget. In fact, in the first 6 years I was in business, I doubt that my budget was more than 0.000001% of theirs. Now, it's probably 0.000002%. So I did the next best thing...

I spoofed them.

Satire, spoofs and commentary are powerful tools. There's an automatic association with the subject of the spoof. Satire is protected under copyright laws, so there is a lot of leeway about poking fun at a brand without any legal repercussions. Every dollar that they spend making "the real thing" visible and part of pop culture makes your take on it more effective and relevant.

Careers have been built on spoofs: from Weird Al to Mel Brooks. Long standing magazines have been created for it such as *MAD Magazine* and *The Onion*. Most of *Saturday Night Live's* good sketches have been goofs on real things, like the Bass-o-Matic as a stand-in for all the goofy kitchen gadgets sold on TV in the late 70s and 80s.

So when Apple's neon colored commercials with silhouettes of dancers in the foreground became some of the most familiar commercials on TV, I knew I had to jump on the bandwagon. Their people were my people. Satire was the tool.

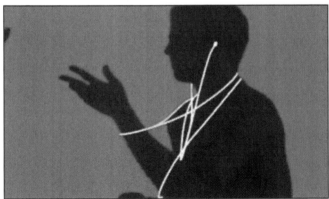

Watch it here - www.scottevest.com/ipodspoof

The iPod Spoof

The idea came to me pretty quickly. All of the Apple dancers had headphone wires dangling all over the place, and in real life, they'd wind up tangled at best, and tear an ear off at worst. We were going to show a before and after: a dancer getting wrapped up in their headphone cords, and then SCOTTeVEST giving them a better way to carry their iPod and earbuds.

It was pretty perfect. Since the dancers were in silhouette, I didn't need to hire an expensive model. There was no set to find or build. Everything was so stylized that I didn't need to worry about lighting or using the best cameras. I even had a video guy who could create it, and for a really decent price.

Being a former lawyer, I paused. This was going to be such a direct imitation of the Apple style that I didn't want to get blindsided by a cease and desist from Steve Jobs. I ~~spent~~ wasted more money on my lawyers looking into the parody question than I spent making the video. The conclusion of the legal review? It was worthless to have the lawyers check it out. This was clearly a parody. Last time I ever made that mistake...

...but it wasn't the last mistake I made on this project. In fact, I have very few regrets in life, but this is one of them. I had an opportunity for Steve Wozniak, co-founder of Apple, to appear in the spoof video, and I didn't take it.

Woz had been a fan of SCOTTeVEST for awhile (I'll tell that full story in chapter 5), and when I told him about the plans for the spoof, he volunteered to be the dancer. I think I already had a vision in my head about what the commercial should be and shouldn't be, and I told him no. This might be my biggest misjudgment of all time.

The video got a lot of views and was the most watched iPod spoof on YouTube for years, but Woz would have taken it to the next level and made it not just watchable, but forward-able. I think he could have been the viral factor.

Years later, I would get a second bite at the Apple - uhhh, the apple - with Woz when we did a series of parody videos together called Woz-i-sodes. More on that later.

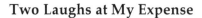

Two Laughs at My Expense

Over time, I've done a lot of parodies. Many of them were spoofs of Apple, and not just because they are a huge brand with a lot of popular appeal, but because I genuinely like and respect their products and approach. We did a take-off on their "There's an App for That" campaign with our "There's a Pocket for That" video and theme song.*

When we launched one of our most innovative products - the Transformer - I did a very Steve Jobs-ian keynote speech, complete with a huge audience. Well, at least the sounds of a huge audience.

While all of those were great pieces to create, I didn't feel like I was making a splash in pop culture until SCOTTeVEST and I were the subjects of some real humor.

As a kid, I would sneak copies of *MAD Magazine* into class so I could read them instead of doing my schoolwork, and now as an adult I'm in it? What could be cooler?

---

* www.scottevest.com/tapft

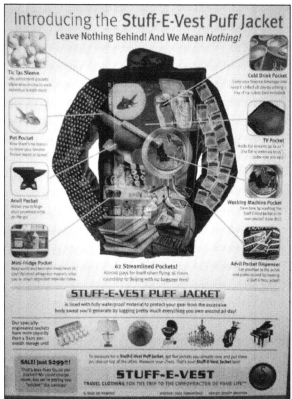

MAD Magazine spoof of a SCOTTeVEST ad

How about *Saturday Night Live* spoofing my appearance on *Shark Tank* as "the vest guy"? While I think Kevin Hart is, um, too short to convincingly play me, the sheer number of messages I received that Saturday night convinced me that I was indeed the subject.

I will gladly be the butt of (almost) any joke as long as they spell my name right.

Going There

I'm always willing to "go there." You know... there. The place where most people aren't willing to go. The place where most people who have worked long and hard enough to become a

CEO would never dare to go. I'm willing to push the boundaries of propriety and common decency.

As a passionate promoter, I'm willing to go too far to make sure that I go far enough.

Surprisingly few people are willing to do that, but the ones who dare are the ones we remember. Could you ever imagine seeing an executive from a major company walking around in his underwear? I did.

After years of making vests, jackets, shirts, hats and pants, it was time to tackle boxer shorts. Travelers were a big part of our clothing market, and travel boxers were a big part of the travel clothing market. We needed to do boxers, and they needed to have pockets. But what's the most innovative way to launch them?

We could hire some hunky underwear models, but how many dozens of other companies have done that?

We could go the lazy route and pop them on a mannequin, but why would anyone care?

We decided that we had to make it fun, and I wanted to make the point clear that these were not only boxers, but could work as shorts, too. I not only posed for photos in my boxers, but created a video where I walked around the office and the downtown neighborhood near our HQ wearing them.

I don't know the meaning of the word embarrassed, but it really didn't even come up in this case. The goal was to get some attention for the new product as the "SCOTTeVEST CEO Exposed" and I thought it would be pretty uncommon to see a CEO in his boxers. It got a lot of eyeballs and it got a lot of people to talk about the boxers, and then buy them. We still sell a ton of them today, and while it wasn't because of my rippling abs, that initial pop of attention got the ball rolling.

It was unique, a little awkward, somewhat controversial and all around a product launch. We even did a more involved follow-up video with more of a storyline, and lots more gratuitous boxer-wearing. My good friend and advisor Hap Klopp (founder of The North Face) agreed to appear as well.

I didn't only decide to do the video because I was feeling "thinspired" and had just lost a lot of weight. I showed off my waist again a few years later when I was the heaviest I've been in a promo for our expandable "Fiesta Waistband" feature.*

Through thick and thin, I'll go there.

What Day Is It?

I love April Fools Day. I'm not really much of a prankster "in real life," but there's something cool about the one day a year that even companies and brands can have some fun. It's a lot more common now, but SCOTTeVEST has been doing crazy things for April 1st since almost the very beginning.

SCOTTeVEST and TEC Acquired for $100 Million!
Playmate to Take over Reins

Chicago – **April 1, 2003** -- Chicago-based Jordan Global Enterprises (JGE), a venture capital firm with diversified holdings, has acquired controlling interests in SCOTTeVEST LLC (SeV) and Technology Enabled Clothing LLC (TEC). The deal was consummated today in all stock deal valued at over $100 million. Jordan Global Enterprises divested itself of large interests in Microsoft, General Electric and other leading companies to acquire SeV and TEC.

---

* Watch my boxer video at www.scottevest.com/exposed

According to Scott Jordan, President/CEO of JGE, "We have been watching SeV and TEC for awhile. We believe that the patent pending Personal Area Network (P.A.N.) will be incorporated into all upper body garments in coming years, making this a billion dollar proposition. We believe the purchase price of $100 million is a bargain." Jordan cited SeV's huge growth earnings – over 1,500 percent increase in revenue last year – as another asset that made the company an attractive buy. "We were drawn to its great earning potential."

You can see the rest at www.scottevest.com/aprilfools

If nothing else, it's an excuse to issue a press release, communicate that your brand doesn't take itself so seriously and in some cases, get "accidental" coverage. A couple blogs picked up on the story as real news, and I even received some congratulatory emails from friends... until they realized the joke was on them.

In the years since, we've usually done something simple like Photoshopping a fake product, and offering a discount on all our real products at the same time. One year it was a hideous SCOTTeVEST jumpsuit. One woman emailed our Customer Service to inform us that she appreciated the joke, but was deleting the email before her husband saw it... because he would want one. We also created the SCOTTeVEST Zero, which would have been the first SCOTTeVEST without any pockets.

One of our main resellers is the website ThinkGeek. We know them well, and have done a ton of business with them over the years. Their fan base can be even geekier than ours, and they need to be extremely careful about making clear which items are for April Fools, and which are real. (Some of the real items they sell sound like they could be jokes.)

It's a great excuse to flex your creative muscles, do something fun and have something to talk about.

Put a New Spin On an Old Idea

Sometimes all you need is a new twist on a current product, or a new way of looking at it. There was a time in 2004 when solar panels were all the rage with gadget people. I heard a few comments from people that we should do a solar jacket. Sometimes, whether an idea is good or bad, all you need is to hear it a few times in a short period of time before it sounds good enough to try.

We were working with a clothing designer at the time, and it seemed like a simple thing to create a way to hang a solar panel from the epaulets that were already built into one of our jackets. After some research about the best semi-flexible solar panels on the market, the SeV Solar Jacket was born.

Some people might say it was just jumping on a bandwagon, and that it was just a publicity stunt. Yes. Yes it was.

The Solar Jacket was covered by dozens of blogs and news outlets. It was even featured in great segments on CNN, NBC's *Today Show*, and in *Newsweek* in China. The exposure was amazing. If you Google "solar jacket" to this day, you'll see references to us on the first page of results.

At about the same time, we started to work with a company called Eleksen, which created "soft controls" for iPods. Imagine a rubbery panel of small buttons that could be sewn into the sleeve of a jacket that would connect to a device in a specific pocket. That was what Eleksen made, and together we developed the SCOTTeVEST Tactical VC Jacket featuring their Elektex buttons.*

Another company - a big company - Kenpo was also using the Eleksen soft controls in some of their products, and they invested millions to advertise it at that year's MAGIC show for the apparel industry. They had huge banners that covered the sides of the whole building in Vegas. It looked like something Microsoft could have done for a major product launch, and easily cost them millions of dollars.

---

* www.scottevest.com/tacticalpr

It was going to be the year that electronics and clothing finally meshed together permanently! Yeah, right.

I'm glad Kenpo spent all that money and not me. Even with all the press for the solar jacket and the soft control jacket, we could hardly sell through the 150 units we made. It was then that I followed my gut to not pursue integrating electronics into my clothing, but to provide the "beige box" into which the customer could put their own devices; whatever they wanted to carry. It proved out, time and again since then.

Once again, I was reminded that press does not always equal sales, and creating a new version of something doesn't guarantee them, either.

We discovered that there were both pros and cons to having versioned products. Yes, it provides a clear reason for people to buy more, but after a while, I realized it might cause people to hold off from buying something NOW if they knew an updated version would come out in a few months.

It turned out, when you start selling directly to the consumer, there is no real need for built-in obsolescence if your products are good enough. Now, we are able to buy three years' worth of a product, realize lots of efficiencies and savings up-front, and be confident that our products won't go out of style.

We're turning fashion on its head by not playing the typical fashion game. Buyers and sellers push fashion and turn the public - well, the parts of the public who care - into fashion slaves. We prefer customers who have their own style (like us), and who appreciate that function is as critical as looks. In many ways, we're the anti-Abercrombie.

Bottom line: you need to try different things to see what works best for you, but more press is always better than none.

Be Timely

Is timing everything? Yes, but only if the time is NOW.

I always hear a clock ticking from the time I wake up in the morning until I crash at night. It's how I've been able to cram two years' worth of progress into one year of time. It can be hard for people to keep up, but when they do, they're amazed by what we can accomplish.

Equally important: timing. As in, the best timing is doing things NOW that need to be done now.

Since pretty much the eVEST 1.0, there had always been a pocket large enough to put a full sized magazine or large book into every SCOTTeVEST. We called this feature the book pocket, the PubPocket™ and probably a few other names as the situation required. Need to carry your best friend? It's a Pup Pocket. The point is that it was big and versatile enough to carry a wide variety of things.

Then, the iPad came out. There were inklings of it in the news. We knew it would be a tablet, we knew when Steve Jobs would be announcing it, and we knew that every single one of our gadget-toting customers would buy one. Or at least want one. The only thing we didn't know… would it fit in our biggest pocket?

My gut said that it probably would. It was worth the gamble. I grabbed a magazine and posed for some photos in our flagship vest putting the magazine into the interior pocket. Our graphic designer was at the ready, beads of sweat rolling down his forehead from the anticipation. Ok, slight exaggeration.

We streamed Steve Jobs' keynote in the office. Damn, that iPad looked cool. It was impressive and it looked pretty small. Of course, all the traffic to the Apple site crashed it, made it slow and barely responsive, but we got onto the iPad page within minutes of it going live. Apple is great like that.

The dimensions of the iPad were listed right there on the page (again, as Apple always does). We knew the maximum size it could be and still fit because we calculated everything ahead of time. "Fits in Men's Vests size Medium and up." Perfect.

A right-click/save image and we had a beautiful photo of the iPad that was debuted to the world less than an hour before. The magazine in my hand became an iPad. The image became a homepage slide. And SCOTTeVEST became the first clothing line in the world compatible with the iPad.

We rode on Apple's coattails. The image of me putting an iPad into the vest pocket went live within an hour, and the press release went out the next day. *The Wall Street Journal* picked it up later, and every tech blogger and writer and gadget freak wanted to know how I got my hands on one the day of the official launch.

I just smiled and rode Apple's wave.

Don't Phone It In

Sending personalized videos probably has the highest ROI of any personal promotion tactic, but there is no substitute for getting out and seeing your fans, supporters and sometimes even the press. But let's make something clear: going to trade shows and being on your feet can suck. Having an audience/fan base that is completely unaware of the passion that fuels your brand is immeasurably worse.

I've been to a lot of trade shows, from my first in Orlando to Comdex to the Consumer Electronics Show (CES) to at least a dozen travel-related shows across the US. In 2013-2014 there was a period of time when I had a show just about every week for a month!

Initially, it was too expensive for me to have a space at most shows. Even still, it's not worth the cost much of the time. At a massive show like CES where some global brands will drop a million bucks on a killer three story tall display, what am I supposed to do? Sit in a 10x10 square in the basement? Reminds me too much of selling cemetery plots.

If a show is "too big" it may be better to walk around and meet the press. It comes down to cost and getting the most out of your time, even more so than getting the most out of your money. Oh, and don't forget that every trade show has a press room, and usually a press lounge. You can't get in there as an exhibitor, but who do you think is constantly streaming in and out of there to get free coffee instead of overpriced, watered-down, trade show floor coffee? That's right, the press. If you're going to a show to hang out and meet people, that's the best place to do it.

Doing a Show in Style

The parts I hate about trade shows are pretty consistent. The standing. The logistics. The set up. The break down. In the beginning, I handled all of it with Laura's help. Now, I have employees to do that, and some of them have even gotten pretty efficient at it. Sometimes, we would be able to outfit the press because SCOTTeVEST is great for the kind of things they need to do and to carry, particularly photographers. As long as they were clear how they got the gear in a review, there was no conflict of interest. They'd even get me press badges to get into special events from time to time as a thank you.

So that leaves me to do all the parts I love about trade shows. Hint: they all involve promotion and sharing my passion for my products. This is my formula for a successful trade show:

- Press Release(s). If it's important enough for me to schlep myself across the country, it's important enough for people to know I'm doing it. Press always covers trade shows, and they usually make a list of booths they want to visit. If they received your press release, you have a better shot of being on their list to visit. Don't ever make them ask for images. Include links to download both high-res and low-res images, and make them super easy to find.

- Super basic: The booth needs to look professional and provide a great backdrop for photos. The logo and company name need to be big enough to be seen from far away, and everything needs to be well lit and well branded. We have an awesome booth setup, and one person can get it up and running in about an hour if they know what they're doing. It was worth the investment.

- My personal vest fully loaded with everything I actually carry. I'm not only demonstrating my products, but I'm using them as intended.

- Crowd control. As much as I love doing an impassioned demonstration fifty times a day, I'd rather do it twenty times to larger groups of people and save my voice.

- Press and influencer meetings. If I'm traveling from Sun Valley, Idaho where we are now based to any major city, you better believe I'm going to meet with everyone I know there and maximize the trip. Breakfast, lunch, dinner, coffee or just a plan to step aside at the show and connect are all great opportunities. You don't need to make a big deal of it, and if you have strong enough relationships with influencers in a city, why not bring them all together for a meal and introduce them to each other? It's at that point that I step out of the spotlight, let the conversation go where it will, and pick up the tab. Believe me, it's not only great fun, but a great way to build relationships and maintain them for years.

- Good food. It's a reward for making it through a long day.

- Fan events. If there is a "secret sauce" to my success at trade shows, it's that I always, always, always schedule at least one fan event to coincide with the show. We start weeks before and email everyone within a zip code sorted circumference of the show that we will be in town. We get feedback on the best place to have a happy hour/apps type of event, and we book it. A week before the event, we send a reminder, then the day before, then the day of. Door prizes. Drinks. Appetizers. Photo opportunities. Promo codes. Show and tell of current and prototype products. Tagging photos on social media and encouraging them to do the same. Thank you emails to all attendees the next day. We do it all. People love meeting the CEO. This type of fan event won't necessarily work for a massive company like Microsoft, but for a passionate promoter, this type of experience is very effective. Fans want to meet the people who started it.

Some of my favorite moments at SCOTTeVEST have been at fan events, and that's not too surprising since some of my favorite moments overall have been interacting with fans.

My craziest (in a good way) fan interaction happened in 2009 at Disneyland, and if I didn't capture it on video, I wouldn't expect you to believe it. Actually, if I didn't capture it on video, I would probably think I had hallucinated it.

Laura and I had just arrived, and (of course) I was recording a selfie-style video blog post. A Disney tour truck was driving by at just that moment, and the tour guide/driver recognized me and called out to me. I chased him down Main Street, USA and had a conversation with him about SCOTTeVEST while he explained to his passengers who I was and they all turned to watch me.

The looks on their faces were somewhere between confused and awe-struck. Laura even recognized who he was from previous interactions. It was one of the strangest, coolest, most gratifying things to ever happen to me… and you need to see the video to believe it.*

With a reception like that, why wouldn't I stack the deck when I travel to make sure that I'm surrounded by fans?

---

* www.scottevest.com/disney

It's cool to mix friends and fans, as well. I did that in Chicago where I used to live, and coincided a fan event with my college reunion in Cincinnati. My friend Christian Payne aka Documentally helped set up a get-together in London for the UK fans.

Each event is different, and the more you plan, the higher the expectation... so don't plan them too much. I always wanted the events to be formulaic, but they really need to be organic based on the crowd, the space, the city, etc. As long as the location is conducive to conversation, you're halfway there. We've done a few fan events at the Thirsty Bear in San Francisco for that reason.

At trade shows, and especially at fan events, the interaction of the fans with each other is as important as them seeing your passion. When I traveled to Australia to give a keynote speech at a conference, we planned a fan event in Sydney and one in Melbourne. There were fans traveling from hours away, not just to meet me, but to meet and interact with other SCOTTeVEST fans. We had a great time, and it was all in the context of my brand.

I feed off the fans' energy. I was lucky enough to be in the audience for a taping of *The Colbert Report*, and just being there was invigorating.

Being on the receiving end of it is even better. But it's important to give even more than you take. Over the years, I've developed real friendships with some "super fans" to the point where I invited them to my 50th birthday party this year... and they're coming.

It doesn't feel like shameless self-promotion if your fans are your friends.

Just Tell People What You Are Doing

Even though I've never really been as low as I was before I started SCOTTeVEST, I do get into a funk every once in awhile and don't know exactly what to talk about. My passionate promotion mojo dial goes from 11 down to 7.4. I think of it as my suckitude level. From 1 to 100, what percentage of "suck" did I experience today? Maybe it's been awhile since our last new product launch. Maybe I just had too much fun on a trip and it's over. Perhaps the "next greatest thing" fell flat.

Whatever it is, personal promotion is a year-round sport, and I get creative to get things moving again.

McDonald's is my favorite restaurant. I'm not shitting you. One day in 2013, we had the idea of figuring out how many pockets we had sold in the history of SCOTTeVEST, like McDonalds old signs for "Billions and Billions Served." It took a few hours of number crunching, but we came to a figure: 9.8 million... and counting. This was a perfect thing to talk about, and it wouldn't be long before we hit 10 Million... which we did... which I promoted.*

A number of years ago, we had an entire container of SCOTTeVESTs stolen from the Port of L.A. Police reports and insurance claims followed, but I didn't feel like the cops were doing enough to actually **catch** the crooks. They weren't. Because we've sold lots of SeVs over the years to federal law enforcement, I have some great contacts, and turned to them for advice.

---

* www.scottevest.com/10million

111

Whoever stole the jackets had to do something to turn them into cash, which meant they would probably sell them on eBay.

I got a little fixated on catching them. I set up Google Alerts for eBay listings and I scoured it every day for weeks. Since the jackets were all from the same numbered batch, it wasn't hard to tell if a jacket that appeared for sale was one of the stolen ones. But ultimately, the thieves were never brought to justice and it still really pisses me off.

But I did learn something. eBay is actually a great secondary market for goods. We developed a plan - a complicated plan - to incentivize our customers to sell their old SCOTTeVESTs on eBay, and buy a new one. We gave them a discount code, and one to share with whoever bought their used SeV. We provided all the graphics and correct descriptions for them to make their eBay listings.

We sent a press release, got some great feedback and coverage, and launched the program.

It fell short of my financial goals, but we got to develop it with input from Jeremiah Owyang, one of the leaders in the Collaborative Economy movement. It was an intriguing experience, and it gave me something to talk about, something to try, something to exercise my passion again.

Even when I swung for the fences and thought that being in *TIME Magazine* would solve all my problems, I was wrong. I never imagined I'd be spoofed in *MAD Magazine* or on *SNL*, and I was.

The most important part of promotion is to do it consistently, and remember that at the end of the day...

Personal promotion is pretty simple. Don't overthink it.

CHAPTER 4
Embrace Controversy

Somewhere between the eVEST 1.0 and the 3.0 Plus, Laura and I decided we had enough of Chicago and it was time for a change.

The company was hitting its stride, and it felt like we turned the corner when *PARADE* magazine covered the eVEST 1.0 in January 2002.∗ As many times as I had built up my expectations in front of an article release only to be let down, I was taken by surprise by the *PARADE* article. I hadn't expected it to give us as big a response as we received from it, and it became the gift that kept on giving.

Exposure to 29 million people at once is going to have some sort of an impact. Even if 99% of people ignore you, you've just increased your audience by 300K. We were able to generate $200-300K in sales in one month, when that could have been our whole year. Even better, we had already launched the eVEST 2.0 before *PARADE*, so our second product was in full view of our new fans.

It felt like a tipping point, and it opened the floodgates to getting lots of press, media attention and sales. We did half a year's business in six weeks. It wasn't SCOTTeVEST's first win, but it was clearly our biggest win up to that time. It set us on a better trajectory.

∗ www.scottevest.com/parade

BY LAMAR GRAHAM

The Gadget Guide
Tools For High-Tech Living

Geek Chic

Clothing is finally catching up to the Digital Revolution with the SCOTT eVEST (about $100; *www.scottevest.com*). Similar to a fisherman's vest, though more stylish, the eVEST contains 15 pockets for electronic gizmos— cell phone, pocket music player, handheld computer, pager, etc.—as well as keys, business cards, tickets, even beverages. For students, photographers and travelers, it's ideal for speeding through airport security: Simply slip off the vest and pass it through the X-ray machine. The

Sites You'll Like

•Linkdup.com
Interested in the art of interactive design? This site by Preloaded, an English firm, provides links to some of the most interesting, innovative and aesthetically challenging sites on the Web.

•familybusinessonline.org
Visit this site from the Austin Family Business Program at Oregon State University to see a streaming-video presentation on how federal tax-law changes enacted in 2001 will affect family businesses. Real Player plug-in is required.

The SCOTT eVEST has enough pockets to hold everything but the kitchen sink.

coolest feature is its Personal Area Network, a series of conduits hidden in the fabric that connect the various pockets to the collar of the vest: Thread your wires through them, and you can wear headphones and headsets without getting tangled up.

Circa January 2002

Months after *PARADE*, toward the end of 2002, SCOTTeVEST had two employees. I still had all the problems that small businesses had, including the really annoying, stupid stuff like dealing with the phone company and getting my printer to work. Seriously, I've wasted 800 hours on those two things since I started SCOTTeVEST. Don't sweat the small stuff, my ass.

But despite the day-to-day frustrations, things were going well. I was able to pay myself a real salary... well, almost. We headed into the 2002 holiday season with good press, and we were featured in some magazine and TV Gift Guides. To this day, I always target Gift Guide writers with press releases and samples each October. It's not always measurable how effective a Guide placement is, but we had crafted a winning formula of presenting SCOTTeVEST as the ultimate gift for gadget lovers.

We wanted this to be the last winter we spent in Chicago.

Fast forward a few months and Laura and I were redecorating the house, and she had an offer to sell her family business (a private school in Chicago). Winter 2003 was coming. (Yes, I'm a huge *Game of Thrones* fan.) No icy zombies on the march, though. It was a Chicago winter, and they're even more fun than they sound, lake effect snow and all. Thanks Canada.

Perhaps now the time was right for us to make good on something we had first discussed years ago on what we still refer to as...

The Compromise Honeymoon

Laura and I were married in January 1996 while I was working at Rudnick/DLA Piper as a lawyer. Working at a law firm, there would never be another chance in my career to take three full weeks off, so there was a lot riding on our honeymoon. We knew we had to make it count, because if we did something lame, Laura knew she would never hear the end of it.

Of course, it was my idea that we go scuba diving. I had been certified since I was a teenager. There's nothing like being underwater. It's still. It's quiet. It's the opposite of how I live my life, and for me, it's a temporary escape from reality. It was going to be a scuba honeymoon!

Until I told Laura.

She was NOT a scuba diver. In fact, she had never gone beyond swimming and snorkeling. She was a skier, and had her sights set on a ski honeymoon. It was January, after all.

I had skied a little in Ohio, but that was very different from what she had in mind. Skiing in the eastern U.S. is mostly ice skiing, and Laura was used to the big, powdery bowls of Deer Valley, Utah and Sun Valley, Idaho. Let's face it, skiing in Ohio is more like going on an icy slip-n-slide than what any avid skier would think of as skiing. Right away, Laura took Sun Valley off the table. I was apparently a beginner, and Sun Valley would be too tough for me. We'll see about that....

Ultimately, we reached a compromise, and it became forever known as "The Compromise Honeymoon." We would spend 2 weeks in Hawaii, and 1 week in Deer Valley. I was psyched... I thought I won 2 to 1! She would learn to scuba, and I would learn to ski. But Laura always plays the long game.

Laura took scuba lessons at night in Chicago (while planning a wedding, of course... no big deal, right?). We wound up going to a murky lake in Wisconsin for her to get her open water certificate so she could scuba in Hawaii. At this point, Laura was regularly competing in multi-sport/adventure races. She was amazingly fit (still is), so there was no doubt she could swim and learn the physical skills required to scuba. But she still had to pass the test.

I was concerned about the lack of visibility in the lake, but I was more concerned about the gassy 300 pound guy who was in the water with her for his own certification. The gas from his burrito lunch affected his buoyancy, and he kept floating up and dragging Laura with him. But still, she passed with flying colors, and was officially pre-certified.

We celebrated by spending the night in the nearby Days Inn. Hearing that we were engaged, they even gave us the honeymoon suite... and it looked like a stuffed cheetah exploded all over the room. There were cheetah print rugs, cheetah print lampshades (with red bulbs, of course). The tackiest thing I've ever seen, and I used to work in New Jersey. (Calm down, Garden Staters, I know you can take a joke.)

When we made it out to Hawaii on the honeymoon, we had a great time. We visited the surf shop that Jerry Garcia dived with, and that was the only reason she felt comfortable. The diving was great. We went on an underwater cave dive the first day, and of course we saw a shark. Laura was fine, but it freaked me out. It turns out that after all the training and certification, we never sent in Laura's paperwork for full certification, and it didn't matter a bit.

116

We had chosen Deer Valley, Utah for phase two of the honeymoon because Laura knew the people there take good care of you. I signed up for lessons, and despite grabbing the wrong rental skis that were sized for a 12 year old, and starting off in three feet of powder on the first day, I had a blast.

Skiing was in our future.

Ski Sun Valley

My next ski trip was with law partners from my firm, and it was not nearly as much fun as my honeymoon. Go figure. But still, I enjoyed skiing more and more each time I went, and I started to get pretty good at it.

Laura had challenged me?... promised me?... that when I was "good enough," she would take me to ski Sun Valley, Idaho. She went there a lot, and had been in SV with her mom when I was in the hypnotherapist's office on the phone with Hammacher. It was her favorite place to ski, but she told me it was a tough mountain and not a good mountain to learn. I accepted her challenge and I was going to hold her to her promise. I was going to become a great skier out of some combination of determination, love, and spite.

After our honeymoon, Laura and I went to a different ski resort for one week each year—Deer Valley, Crested Butte, Big Mountain, Aspen. My skiing improved with each trip, but I also gained an appreciation for the lifestyle in these mountain resort towns. It got my gears turning… could I be like Jerry Spence, the lawyer and political pundit who was featured frequently in the national media, but still lived in Jackson Hole, Wyoming?

Why not! I applied to some law firms in ski towns, but no bites. Still, there was something drawing me to living in a town like these, and Laura was on board… but she said it had to be Sun Valley. Within a few years, I was deemed to be skilled enough to conquer SV, and I was allowed to go with her and see what all the fuss was about. Ok, maybe not to conquer it, but at least not to die on the side of the Mt. Baldy.

We landed in the cramped prop plane at the dinky single-gate airport about a 12 minute drive from the mountain. Walking down the steps onto the tarmac - yeah, you climb in and out of the plane yourself - I couldn't deny that it was beautiful. But it was just such a pain in the ass to get there.

Turns out, that's part of the appeal.

It was where Hemingway made his home and where he took his life. It's much smaller than Vail, more secluded and protected, less transient, and has much better restaurants. There are no chain stores, other than one Starbucks that was allowed by an act of Congress. (Only a slight exaggeration.)

Sun Valley photo by Thomas Hawk

There's a real sense of community there. The person next to you on a ski lift could be a ski bum or a movie producer, and they'll strike up a conversation with you just the same. Even though Laura and I were not practicing Jews, there was something intriguing about the fairly big Jewish community in Sun Valley.

People who come to Sun Valley come back year after year, and many people who buy a vacation home wind up moving to SV full time.

Living in Sun Valley

At this point, you may be wondering when the controversial part is going to occur. Your wait is over. It was 2003, and we went out to Sun Valley to look for places to live.

There were no business reasons for moving to Idaho, and in fact, other places would have been more advantageous. At this point, SCOTTeVEST had been successful for over 2 years, and we were growing steadily. We had sold over a hundred thousand pockets by then.

Sun Valley photo by Thomas Hawk

To bring the business to Sun Valley I would need more of an incentive than having a good view of the mountain from town. Forget the fact that there isn't any water for speedboats, and no racetracks anywhere in this state.

The potato state. Yeah, that's what Idaho is known for, and if it wasn't so oddly shaped I doubt most Americans could pick it out on the map.

Because there are only 4,006 year round residents of Sun Valley and the neighboring town of Ketchum, it would be hard to recruit employees. Wait, wait, make that 4,005... Jeff Smith just moved out.

At the time, I didn't think much of the small population being a hindrance to recruiting. SCOTTeVEST was a lean machine, and how many people would we really need? It turns out, more than I expected.

Things lined up for us to make a move. Our lease was going to expire. Laura was in the process of selling her business. All our friends were having kids, and as neat as that is, we weren't having any. At least none with two legs and no tail.

It was worth a six month experiment to see if we could live out in Sun Valley full time.

Laura left the final decision up to me, and I passed the message that we were moving to her through the painter that was working on our house at the time. We were in Sun Valley one month later with all our inventory in the garage and some storage units. Six months came and went, and we've never looked back.

Cease and Desist

My name is Scott. Their name is Scott.

I make clothing. They make clothing.

I'm in Sun Valley. They're in Sun Valley.

It was a problem I didn't think I would ever have, but I was being sued for using my own name. And, objectively speaking, I can see why it happened.

Once I started getting real press for SCOTTeVEST, we caught the eye of SCOTT USA, and specifically that of their lawyers. SCOTT USA is a great brand that makes ski equipment... and clothing. I even own and use some of their gear. We were still in Chicago when we got the first letter from their lawyers. Bottom line: they were concerned about consumers confusing my brand for theirs.

Our names both started with SCOTT, but that was pretty much where the similarities ended as far as I was concerned. No one has ever called me up accidentally looking for ski poles or goggles, and I doubt they've gotten any calls looking for pockets. I didn't think the logos were similar enough to be mistaken for each other. I responded to the letter, told them there was no way there could be any confusion, and that if there was we would make it clear immediately that our companies were not connected. I wasn't doing anything remotely related to the ski market.

It's one thing to be associated with a great brand, but I was building my own brand identity, and it didn't behoove me to encourage any confusion in the public eye.

I waited for a response from their legal team, but never received one. Fine by me. I had enough to do, and if they weren't concerned enough to pursue, I wasn't going to push it.

Then I moved to Sun Valley.

After our first six months here, Laura and I put down some roots. We bought a home and rented a small warehouse space for SCOTTeVEST. It wasn't anything fancy, but I put my mark on it: a big, proud SCOTTeVEST sign on the outside of the building.

I was sued within a week.

There was no courtesy call, no letter. I was flat-out served with a lawsuit.

You see... SCOTT USA's headquarters are in Sun Valley. I didn't even realize they were based here until after we moved. It's not like their location was obscured, but it didn't really click for me.

Circa 2004

Unintentionally, my SCOTTeVEST sign looked a little too much like theirs, someone probably saw it driving to work and they pulled the trigger. I was blindsided.

Embracing Whatever Hits Off the Fan

Even though I was a lawyer, I knew I had to get some legal advice. I had my Milwaukee patent attorney's office look into it. Patents and trademarks go hand-in-hand, so it was a good move, and beyond that I really didn't know where else to go. Knowing full well the type of costs that go along with litigation, I did not want this to go all the way to court.

But it did…all the way to federal court. We had to go to the federal courthouse in Boise for mandatory mediation. It was a two hour drive from Sun Valley (well, at my speed), but I was the only one footing legal AND flight bills. They were adding up fast.

Usually big companies - and SCOTT USA definitely qualifies as one - try to keep things like this quiet. They don't like to air their dirty laundry. It can embarrass their investors. It can distract their PR firm from getting them positive press. And every public move they make needs to be approved in triplicate from their legal team.

I'm allowed to do anything I want. That's the advantage of being an entrepreneur. I embraced the controversy.

I forwarded a copy of the lawsuit to the *Wood River Journal*, which is Sun Valley's local newspaper, and they wrote a fantastic article about it titled, "A War of the 'Scotts' Looms."*

They interviewed me about the lawsuit, and I was able to speak a lot more frankly about what I thought was going on than SCOTT USA was able to do. I felt like they were trying to intimidate me out of making a living, and I said so. I very carefully chose my sound bytes, and it all made it to print.

If you've ever lived in a small town with one newspaper, then you know that everyone in town reads it. Every. Single. Person. And then they all talk about it for the next week.

I was David and SCOTT USA was Goliath. I was the small business trying to make it, and they were the international brand trying to squash my dreams, steal all my money, and put me out of business. It was like the big railroad company trying to drive the farmer from his family land. In a frontier town, it rang true. And SHIT, my name is Scott. What was I supposed to do?... change MY name, too?

I became an overnight, local celebrity. I couldn't go to the grocery store without someone stopping me to talk about it. People bought me drinks. By winter, I couldn't get on a ski lift without being asked about the lawsuit. Everyone in town

---

* www.scottevest.com/WRJ

supported my story, and it created a lot of social pressure on SCOTT USA.

Photo by Thomas Hawk

One day, I found myself on the chairlift next to the CEO of SCOTT USA. Awk-ward! Well, awkward for him, but not for me. It wasn't a long conversation, but he did tell me that the pressure to pursue litigation was coming from their parent company in Europe, not the local team. I'm not sure if that was true, but they were proceeding in any case.

Settled

Defending the lawsuit wound up costing about $50K (and costing them a lot more), but the PR value and being cemented into the hearts and minds of the community took some of the sting out of it. I knew every bit of it pissed off the bigwigs at SCOTT USA, and I embraced that, too.

Eventually, we started to make progress.

We wound up going back to essentially what I offered to do in my first letter to them in Chicago: change the logo into something that would make it impossible to confuse us. Through a lot of back and forth, we narrowed in on some details. I would always show the words SCOTT e and VEST together without spacing (SCOTTeVEST), and we would be very, very careful about how we mentioned Sun Valley in connection with our company.

I even threw in that they could have final approval of the logo. They agreed. Of course, if they had agreed when I was still in Chicago, none of us would have had to go through the expenses. There would have been no real controversy to embrace.

Then, over the phone, my lawyer told me one more thing that the SCOTT USA camp wanted. He said, "There's something else. They're insisting that you pay their legal fees, which to date have been approximately $100,000. They simply won't budge on that."

I paused.

Usually, I speak fast. Speed is my language as much as English is. But this time, I wanted there to be no confusion.

I said to my lawyer," write this down, because when you try to give them my response, you're going to find it's pretty complex, and I'm afraid you might miss some of it. I want to make sure you get it all, every word of it, and I want to be absolutely certain that you deliver to them what I say, exactly as I say it. Ready?"

"Sure," he said, with pen at the ready.

I said, "Remember, I'm your client. You **have** to give them this response word-for-word, and you can't change any of the language. Not one word of it."

"Got it," he said.

"You can tell them," I said very slowly, "to suck ... my ... dick. Did you get all that? The words I want you to say to them, out loud, are: Suck. My. Dick."

There was silence on the other end of the phone.

I said, "There's no way on earth that I am going to pay for their idiotic mistake of choosing this forum to settle this dispute. What they are proposing is **exactly** what I proposed to them before we started flying all the lawyers back and forth, with the exception of them wanting me to foot the bill for their screw-up. Tell them to *suck my dick.*"

Whether he actually did say those words or not, I have no idea. But the next thing I heard from him was that I didn't need to pay their fees.

I signed the dotted line. We changed the logo. We were written about in the papers. The controversy, once embraced, was over.

Life went on.

Not My First Rodeo

As big of a deal as the SCOTT USA lawsuit was, it wasn't the first time that SCOTTeVEST had been sued in its first couple years in business. Being a former lawyer, this didn't freak me out as much as it would most business owners, but that also meant that I fully understood the worst-case scenario.

The first time I was the target of a lawsuit was from IBM. Yes, that IBM. The multi-billion, multi-national blue chip stock IBM. They had their sights on me.

The "why" was the dumbest part. It had nothing to do with "y" it had to do with "e" - specifically, the e in the SCOTTeVEST logo.*

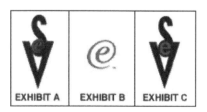

While still in Chicago and trying to establish the SCOTTeVEST brand identity, we tried out a number of logos. To add emphasis to the "e," we settled on a scripted lowercase letter. I thought it

---

* See the full story at www.scottevest.com/IBM

was a great idea, and so did IBM... but they did it first on their e-business logo.

It didn't matter to them that they were a consulting service, and we sold vests and jackets. It was a classic case of the Golden Rule: he who has the gold makes the rules. IBM probably had more lawyers on staff than I had customers at the time. So what did I do?

I embraced controversy.

It wasn't about IBM sending me a letter. It was about Goliath brazenly challenging David. They had letter-writing pens (mightier than swords in this case) and an army of lawyers, and I had a rock and a sling. At least my ass wasn't in the sling, not yet.

I was faster than they were. I could say things quickly without getting my statements cleared through seven layers of approvals. I could speak directly to the press. I could answer questions truthfully based on how I really felt, and not just a script. And most importantly: while they had hundreds of legal actions going on at any time, I only had one. I wasn't going to lose it.

Big companies aren't allowed to embrace controversy. I was, and used that to my advantage.

I told everyone about the IBM letter. I sent out press releases and emailed my customers and fans. Some styles of eVESTs with the "illicit e" started to sell out... people thought they'd become collector items if things got serious between IBM and my young company.

Ultimately, I knew that I would change the e. I wasn't all that attached to it, and my lawyer estimated it would cost a million bucks to fight it. Principle is one thing, but fighting this lawsuit in court would put me out of business.

I had decided that I wasn't going to spend a million fighting it. I was going to make a million by telling the world about it.

David v. Goliath

You probably can't afford a legal battle with a big company, so strategy is key

BY SANDRA SWANSON

Scott Jordan
ScottEVest Inc.

Scott Jordan's company designs garments with special pockets for carrying personal electronics like cell phones, MP3 players and PDAs. It also designed a logo that irked IBM Corp.

In 2001, the company started using a lowercase "e" in ScottEVest that apparently resembled the "e" in IBM's e-business logo.

Mr. Jordan, 40, didn't notice the similarity, but he definitely noticed the cease-and-desist letter in spring 2002 from a law firm for IBM, saying his "e" was violating IBM's trademark. "I immediately freaked out and forwarded it to my attorney," says Mr. Jordan, himself a former Chicago lawyer.

Mr. Jordan's lawyer told him IBM didn't have a case because its "e" was registered under consulting services, while Mr. Jordan's "e" applied to clothing. But the attorney also told him he'd need $1 million to fight IBM.

Mr. Jordan caved and agreed to change the font. "I could have dug in my heels, and it would have ruined the business," he says.

But he did turn the tiff into a public relations blitz. He circulated a press release about the settlement and included the story in his e-newsletter, which has 40,000 subscribers.

People started calling to order any remaining clothing with the illicit "e," thinking they would become collectors' items.

▶ TAKEAWAYS

If you think another company is doing something inappropriate, have your lawyer send the firm a **cease-and-desist** letter.

If a company demands that *you* stop doing something, weigh the **cost of doing battle** carefully—it may not be worth a fight.

Crain's Chicago Business

In the end, we ceased and desisted. It cost us hundreds of dollars (yeah, just hundreds) to reprint hangtags, and about thirty bucks to update the logo on the website. We've updated that logo at least ten more times since then, and never used a stupid script lowercase e ever again.

The experience with IBM gained us dozens of articles and mentions, positioned us as "David fighting Goliath" with our customers and fans on our side, helped expose us to generate hundreds of thousands in sales that we might never have seen, and gave me a great story.

So... who really won?

Controversy Doubles Your Opportunities

A lot of people have been conditioned to shy away from uncomfortable situations, but as an entrepreneur, the risks I faced (and conquered) starting SCOTTeVEST prepared me to take on any challenge. I embrace controversy because controversies are opportunities.

If you look at everything you could talk about - product launches, new partnerships, seasonal promotions - they are all positive events. Sometimes, negative situations can be turned into even bigger positive events because there is added drama, energy and interest in that conversion.

You double the amount of opportunities if you consider negative opportunities as opportunities, too.

There can be a fine line between taking advantage of a negative situation - particularly one that has been thrust upon you - and basic internet trolling. How have I kept that distinction? I've always been clear about my goals and intentions, and understand that the process (and documenting it) is usually much more important than the outcome.

Embracing controversy allows you to play the long game.

You Never Know What Could Go Viral

As much as I'm always on the lookout for opportunities to promote myself - whether they are controversial or not - sometimes, things just fall into your lap. Sure, you might do something that accidentally catches the eye of a big corporation like IBM and results in a lawsuit. You might even get served because the name you were born with was already in use by another company, and you happened to love where they are based.

But sometimes... it's like this shit just falls from the skies. I'm always ready to catch it and run with it.

Starting back in 2010, we were buying a fair amount of print ads in magazines. *The New York Times Travel Magazine, Sunset Magazine, Smithsonian* and some specialty publications. We bought everything as "remnant" ads, which meant that we could save 90%+ off the normal cost of a print ad in a magazine if a) we bought it "at the last minute" and b) we weren't picky about what page in the magazine it ran.

It was a marketing strategy that worked really well for over a year before losing its effectiveness, and right in the middle of the successful part of the run, we had a great idea: airline magazines.

Every airline has its own magazine. I'm not talking about *SkyMall*, which I have strong opinions about, but will save for another book. I mean the airline magazines: *United Hemispheres*, Air Canada's *Enroute Magazine*, Delta's *Sky Magazine*. Our products were great for travelers, so it seemed like a natural fit. What better way to tell travelers about how our multi-pocket clothing makes traveling cheaper and easier, than to tell them while they were in the act of traveling.

We jumped on the idea. My graphic designers put together a simple, but effective ad that hit all the points we wanted to make.

Circa October 2010

This was not the first print ad we had done, and this was not even the first print ad we had done with this messaging. It wasn't the first print ad we did for an airline magazine, and further, it wasn't the first print ad we did for an airline magazine with this messaging.

Basically, this was nothing new. We weren't stirring any pots. This wasn't engineered to create any controversy, and as such, there was no expectation that it would.

Every ad gets submitted for approval to a publication. Usually, you get a perfunctory "thanks" response, or no acknowledgement at all. Many publications require the artwork to be uploaded through a special website portal that checks your margins and font sizes to make sure it fits the specs required for the magazine.

No one on the magazine end proofreads for spelling or grammar. If there's a typo, it's not their job to tell you. But someone always approves the content. When we submitted the ad to *Delta Sky Magazine*, the process was no different. But the outcome was.

Initially, we submitted a generic ad for approval, but made some copy tweaks to appeal to people who would be sitting on a plane at the time when we turned in the final version. This version is what caused the reaction. For the first time since we had been doing print ads, our ad was rejected based on the content.

Was there some mistake? Did they have a problem with us using the URL www.scottevest.com/DELTA as a way of tracking the traffic from the ad? Some magazines didn't like their name in the URL because it sounded like they were endorsing the company. Whenever that happened, we'd just roll our eyes, change the URL and resubmit.

But that wasn't the problem. They rejected the ad because we said that SCOTTeVEST could help you save on baggage fees. I was pretty incredulous, since it seemed to imply that my pockets were a credible threat to a source of revenue for one of the largest airlines in the world. They even rejected an alternate headline we provided to them, on the same basis.

They were saying that SCOTTeVEST pockets were going to cost the airlines $4 billion (with a B) a year in extra baggage fees, and cripple their profitability. They thought my ad was so controversial that it would blow the minds of travelers, and no airline in the world would be able to charge for extra bags ever again, because all travelers would be carrying their extra stuff in pockets.

We weren't allowed to run the ad in *Delta Sky Magazine* on that basis. Are you kidding me?

The Video

At first, I didn't even recognize this as an opportunity, or even as a controversy. It kind of made me laugh that Delta felt threatened by an ad my creative team wrote in 20 minutes. It was a semi-clever headline and some messaging points. These kind of ads get churned out every day without incident. The situation was ridiculous, and I had to vent.

As I do pretty often, I turned on my camera and recorded a little video. Basically, I thought the situation was ridiculous, and I wanted to post about it on Facebook.*

But then the unexpected happened. It struck a nerve. People got pissed - really pissed - and it wasn't directed at me for a change. "The public" was on my side.

I didn't think my post would amount to anything. It was just a random moment to express myself, and I thought it would be a regular tweet that would get a few replies from my die-hard followers and friends, and then die. We'd either stand on principle and find somewhere else to run it, or we'd make some quick edits. Even if I imagined how it might take off, I couldn't imagine what actually happened.

I received an email from a reporter for *WalletPop* (which was owned by AOL) for an interview. We talked minutes later, and when the article went live, it was on the AOL News homepage. Holy shhhh.....

What followed was a few days of ever-increasing media coverage. We were in *The Huffington Post*, *Forbes Magazine*, CBS News, AOL News, Yahoo News and dozens - literally, dozens - of travel and gadget blogs. The media was fighting our fight. It struck a nerve with writers and with the segment of the pop culture that was tired of being nickel and dimed by airlines.

---

* You can see the video at www.scottevest.com/deltavid

I started to capitalize on the exposure as soon as the first article came out, and we issued a press release immediately. That first article established credibility for my complaint, and proved that even when I was looking for angles to exploit for promotion, sometimes you just don't know what's going to catch fire.

I didn't bait *Delta Sky Magazine* into rejecting the ad. I didn't even think it would be controversial.

The end result was that the controversy generated much more coverage than the magazine would have received sitting in the seat back pockets of Delta flights for four weeks. The Delta team's PR blunders turned into gold, for many of the same reasons I was able to capitalize on the IBM controversy.

It was David and Goliath all over again, and it didn't matter in the end whether the ad ran or not... the ride was worth the price of admission a thousand times over.

As with all news, good or bad, it runs its course. I wished I was able to get even more exposure out of the incident with additional major media interviews. In an attempt to keep it going a little longer, we created a contest with a prize of Delta Sky Miles, which I was generously willing to donate from my own account. We were able to send someone on a lovely trip, but the buzz around the incident was over.

The Delta controversy still gets mentioned from time to time, such as in *The Washington Post* article a few months later that got us an "approval" from the TSA: pockets are not bags. It wasn't something anyone couldn't figure out on their own, but we had the words from an official source.

We could count this one as a victory all around.

The Ultimate Controversy: *Shark Tank*

Anyone who has seen my episode of *Shark Tank* would agree it's the most controversial episode of the entire series, bar none. No other guest up to that point had received the 16 minutes of air time that I got. I say this to you without a hint of irony, without a shadow of doubt… it's an objective fact: my *Shark Tank* appearance polarized the audience and made damn good TV. I was even voted one of the most entertaining segments by the largest unofficial *Shark Tank* blogs.

My episode was Season 3, Episode 7 and debuted on March 2, 2012. If you've already seen it, you remember what happened. I wish there was a free way for me to share it with you all, but there isn't. It is available on iTunes and Amazon* and it was epic. In fact, I don't think someone can call him or herself a fan of the show without having seen it. It was even voted the most polarizing episode by *Shark Tank* Blog. I'm going to give you the full story, but a picture is worth a thousand words and a video is worth a million.

Whether you've seen the episode or not, you're most likely familiar with the show concept. A panel of five very wealthy "Sharks" (or Dragons in the UK and Canadian versions) judge presentations by inventors and entrepreneurs, and decide if they want to invest their own money into the entrepreneur's company. Since this is done on network TV, the entrepreneur's company is exposed to a massive national audience. The sophistication of the entrepreneurs ranges from aww shucks workshop tinkerers to savvy businesspeople.

To be clear, I did NOT present SCOTTeVEST on the show, for reasons that will soon become apparent. SCOTTeVEST was doing great as an internet retail company. What I wanted to do on *Shark Tank* was to realize my **original** dream for the Personal Area Network; the dream that I had from day one.

I went on *Shark Tank* to build the licensing end of my business, and to promote the patented PAN system through TEC-Technology Enabled Clothing®. TEC is a separate entity that has existed for years, and to which SCOTTeVEST pays modest royalties for the use of the PAN system. TEC was, is and will always be set up as a separate company for licensing purposes, and it has already licensed the system to Polo Ralph Lauren, Calvin Klein, The North Face, and many other huge companies.

---

* Links to both are at www.scottevest.com/sharktank

As Seen On *Shark Tank*: All the Parts They Aired

This section gives a shot for shot account of what appeared on the screen in my episode of *Shark Tank* (not necessarily what happened during filming). It is written as if you are watching it on TV. If you haven't seen the episode, this will tell you what it looked like as if you saw it. If you are familiar with my appearance, just skim this section as a refresher before we go behind the scenes in the subsequent parts of this chapter.

The Pitch

The doors of the *Shark Tank* studio open and I walk confidently through them and past the camera into the main room. The voiceover explains that I am Scott Jordan and that I am here to entice the Sharks with the patent to my clothing technology.

The camera shows reaction shots of each of the Sharks - Barbara Corcoran, Robert Herjavec, Daymond John, Kevin O'Leary and Mark Cuban - intercut with my pitch. My ask: $500,000 investment for 15% of my company, TEC-Technology Enabled Clothing®.

As I list off all the gadgets I'm carrying in my pockets at that moment, the camera pans over an identical set of gadgets on the table next to me, in full view of the Sharks. The viewer does not see me unload anything from my 24 pocket travel vest, but I go on to explain how the pockets are engineered to hold every device shown on the table, and that I am carrying it all right there on screen.

I demonstrate some of the special features of the vest, like the clear touch pockets that allow you to see and control your touchscreen device through the clear fabric. The camera continues to cut back and forth between my presentation and the Sharks reactions, and they appear to be listening intently, some of them smiling.

After I mention the patented Personal Area Network and how it can prevent headphones from becoming a tangled web of wires, and my intention to license it to every major clothing manufacturer, the camera cuts to Daymond John as he underlines something on his notepad. The next cut shows him smiling as all of the Sharks pay close attention to the end of my pitch.

I conclude by saying, "I've told you about my pockets. Now it's time for you to reach deep into yours."

The Q&A

Right off the bat, Robert mentions that he was flipping through a magazine and recently saw one of our ads, thinking the product was a great idea. I respond to him that it was indeed our ad, and it is a great concept, but the bigger idea is the intellectual property behind the clothing line that can be licensed to other companies.

He asks about the retail business and how that is doing, since it is a proof of concept for the TEC System. I answer that we are on track to making $12 million dollars this year, and watch as most of the Sharks write that down, and all of them perk up.

When I clarify that the retail business is not part of my appearance on *Shark Tank*, you could hear a pin drop in the studio. The camera cut to the Sharks' reactions and there is some mixture of disappointment and confusion across their faces. I again clarify that the intellectual property of TEC is what is on the table, and a voice over reinforces that again for the home audience.

Kevin chimes in and asks me in his deadpan way why I'm being so "greedy and savage" and not giving them a piece of the retail pie. With a huge, ear-to-ear smile I reply, "because I'm like you!" which got a good laugh from the panel.

Daymond asks the next question, and inquires about the technology they would be investing in. As the founder of FUBU, Daymond is a sharp guy who knows the clothing industry, and he mentions that he has seen brands like Burton use this type of headphone wiring system for years. Of course, he is right, but they had been infringing on my patent, and along with 10 other major corporations - among them The North Face, Polo Ralph Lauren, Calvin Klein - they have settled their infringement by paying me royalties for use of the patent.

At this point, Kevin essentially calls a time out and talks over all the other Sharks. He looks me right in the eye and says, "You need me... I know how to sue people. This is going to be wonderful!... I need it all, though." As jovial as the exchange was, this is when the tone began to shift. I didn't need him for the retail side of my business, and I said that plainly.

Daymond takes over the questioning and asks me to explain exactly what my patent contains. I describe how TEC-Technology Enabled Clothing® owns the intellectual property for the incorporation of third party wires into clothing, and that the patent has not only been issued, not only been tested in litigation, but re-examined and passed re-examination as well.

Other than a few laughs, Mark Cuban has remained quiet until this point.

That changes right now when he shouts, "That is ridiculous! That is just ridiculous! That's just common sense!... that's what's killing this country... dumbass patents!" and throws back his head in disbelief.

I'm taken a little aback, but I keep my cool and try to defuse his outburst. I understand where he's coming from, because the patent IS obvious, but it's also mine. This is when I let it out that I am a former lawyer and hate frivolous litigation.

Cuban fires back, "You're so full of crap!" and Kevin jumps in to try to neutralize his over the top tone. Compared to the pretty light tone of the interactions up to this point, Mark's comments seem disproportionately angry. I try to laugh off having obviously hit a hot button.

Daymond explains how a designer in a clothing business like his might accidentally infringe on a patent, then settle out of court to avoid racking up attorney fees. Kevin jumps in with a gleeful, "I love it!" while Mark keeps shouting, "Horrible! Horrible! Horrible! Horrible!" while pounding his hands together.

This is the point of no return.

I fire back with a fact: creating unique ideas, patenting them, and defending them is what this country is built on.

Reining It In

Everyone on screen seems to take a breath as Robert very calmly takes the reins and restates the facts of what I am offering. Daymond is concerned that without a piece of the retail end of the business, the growth of the licensing end could be eclipsed, and they would be stuck with a piece of a much smaller pie.

I assure him that everything is negotiable. I am here to negotiate.

Robert makes an offer: $500K for 15% of the patent business AND the retail business.

I respond with an incredulous, "You've got to be kidding me... that is insane," which he shrugs off. The math of that deal would mean that my retail business was only worth about $3 million if 15% of it was worth $500K. Yearly sales were over four times that total valuation at the time.

Our exchange is punctuated by cutting to a commercial break.

Back in Action

The final seconds of the exchange are repeated, and I break down the math behind the offer to explain why I must object to it. I explain that I am on the show for their connections, their expertise, their help, and their money.

Barbara speaks for the first time and very politely asks if I have a business partner, because they must be a saint. She acknowledges that I'm tough. I tell the room that my partner is my wife Laura, and Kevin wryly asks if she's a lawyer, too. She is. Everyone - including Mark Cuban - has a laugh.

Barbara says that she is "out," which is how the Sharks on *Shark Tank* say they are not going to make an offer.

The conversation turns to the valuation of my retail company, and the discussion become abstract and speculative. I say that I believe with our sales and growth trajectory, the retail company is worth $30 million.

This prompts Mark Cuban to turn his attention back to my patent, which he attempts to poke holes in by talking about wireless headsets and Bluetooth. I counter his comments, but it doesn't matter. He declares himself "out."

"You were out from the moment you sat down," is my reply. "You're no loss."

It's clear that the Sharks are feeling insulted that they were not given a chance to invest in my retail company, and that is at the heart of the rising tensions. With that, Daymond calls himself "out."

Kevin makes it crystal clear that he "gets it." Even if Mark is right about wireless technologies eroding my market share, there is plenty of money to make until that happens, whether I believe wireless will ever take over or not.

Kevin makes a few offers of his own: he's willing to go in with Robert on the original offer, or if Robert is willing to go in with him, double the offer. In other words, $1 million for 30% of my patent and retail businesses. He is also willing to match Robert's offer if I would rather work with him.

Making the Call

I tell them that I need to make a phone call to speak to someone on my advisory board: Steve Wozniak, co-founder of Apple. Mark and Kevin both want me to say hi to him.

I duck out to make my call to Woz, and the camera shows the Sharks talking amongst themselves. Mark maintains his stance that the patent system is wrong, and in this case, Daymond agrees. Kevin loves it. He smiles almost the whole time.

I explain the situation to Woz, and he agrees that their offer was not enough. Almost every second of our phone call made it to air.

I tell Mark that Woz says hi, and I tell Kevin that Woz says he doesn't know him. It's clear I'm just joking and we have another good laugh.

Endgame

I give the Sharks an opportunity to reconsider their offers, and explain to them what I discussed with Woz: their offers are just too low. I want to give them a chance to make a more reasonable offer, but as we start talking again, it's clear that we are not going to come to an agreement.

At this point, I motion to Kevin and Robert and tell them that they are "out." If this is their best offer, I don't need them. Kevin reminds me that I'm walking away from a million dollars, but it's too late and I am not regretting anything.

Daymond jumps in that he feels like I didn't come to make a deal and I wasted their time. I am shown clapping my hands together, saying "bye bye" and walking out the doors without shaking anyone's hands.

The episode closes with me speaking into the camera. I say, "I went in looking for a deal. I truly did, but unfortunately the valuation they put on my other company combine was just… insulting. I had no other choice. I had to walk."

The credits roll and the episode ends.

The Producer's Cut: All the Things They Didn't Let You See

If you have seen the episode as it aired on ABC, you probably either thought I was an arrogant jerk just looking for free publicity... or hopefully you thought I was a brilliant businessman who would not let the Sharks push me around.

If you haven't seen the episode, you would probably think the same exact thing. In reality, it was a little from column A and a lot from column B, but the way it was stitched together in the editing suite certainly skewed the perception away from "savvy" and toward "obnoxious."

While I wasn't as sweet as Mary Poppins in there, I was no more Sharky than the Sharks. They had just never gotten a taste of their own medicine. If you want to watch, I recorded a couple hours of background information and have it posted at www.scottevest.com/sharktank.

Truth be told, I was nervous. Really nervous. Filming was done in the back of this huge hangar of a studio. Guests got ready in a curtained-off section at one end, and filming took place on the other side. You could have parked a 747 in the space in between. Talk about intimidating.

They had come to get me from the hotel around 4AM, but it wasn't until early afternoon when filming began. That's a lot of time to get lost in your own thoughts. I chatted with another entrepreneur in the waiting area, but we were both going over our own pitches to ourselves again and again and again. Oh yeah, I totally forgot it one time. I know it was just nerves, but that didn't make it any better.

Before you go in for filming, there was a part of the set where they shoot the guest looking nervous and jittery. After being brought there, the producer asked me to act nervous for the camera. Then, she asked me to stop looking so nervous. I felt like Will Ferrell in that *SNL* sketch where he cannot modulate the tone or volume of his voice... but it was my nervousness that couldn't be dialed back. They didn't wind up using any of that footage.

On top of it all, my arm was killing me. I had fractured my elbow the day before, and it was one of the stupidest things I've ever done. I've had this Razor scooter for years, and I thought it would be neat to get a little ride on it with my poodles pulling me down the street. They thought it was lots of fun, and I did too, until I hit a pothole and flew over the handlebars and onto my elbow. At least I didn't lose any teeth.

I tried to shake it off and paced back and forth, racing as fast as my mind was. I almost ran into the janitor who had walked into the path I was pacing into his floors.

"What did you have for breakfast?" he asked. His face was dead serious.

It was a nonsensical question. Was this guy crazy? Was he serious?

"What did you have for breakfast?" he repeated.

"Uhhh... bacon, eggs. Toast. Ummm, coffee."

"Good!" he said, and went about his business. Turns out, it was a test. The producers wanted to make sure I had my wits about me. Some people "pull a deer in the headlights" when they hit the studio, and they wanted to make sure I wasn't going to freak out. It seemed like a possibility at the time.

As soon as I went in to the studio, it was game time, and I was in control. Well, except for when the video monitor with graphics to add punch to my presentation didn't work, and the producers cut me off in the middle of my pitch. Then again. And again. It finally worked, and I was able to get through the initial pitch. The rest would be Q&A.

I did a full demo of the SCOTTeVEST, pulling out just about every gadget and showing off every feature. If they had shown me pulling my stuff out of the vest, it would have changed the future of SCOTTeVEST... but they didn't. It was cut from the final edit.

Now go ahead and ask yourself this: if I'm able to stare down lawyers, walk into the lobbies of the top media companies in the world and passionately promote myself anywhere, anytime... why was I so nervous about being on yet another TV show?

Here's your answer:

At the time of my appearance, there was a rule that was kept secret from the home audience: just for appearing on the show, the producers got 5% of your company or 2% of your profits. It didn't matter if one of the Sharks chose to invest in you or not, or whether your segment ever made it on the air or not. Sign on the dotted line, and you had a 5% partner for life.

This is an incredibly important thing to keep in mind, and it's something that the viewers at home never knew unless they happened to see the above image in the end credits for the fraction of a second it appeared on screen. In fact, the line about this percentage was buried on page 28 of the 32 page contract.

Oh, you can't read the text on that screen shot? Neither can most people. Here it is zoomed in:

SONY PICTURES TELEVISION, A DESIGNEE OF MARK BURNETT, AND ABC MAY RECEIVE EQUITY IN OR A SHARE OF REVENUES GENERATED BY THE BUSINESSES INCLUDED IN THIS PROGRAM.

For the first time since starting SCOTTeVEST, I thought, "Good thing I was a lawyer." I'm sure there was at least one mild mannered inventor who missed that language and is still sending them quarterly checks.

No one's appearance was free. My appearance was not free.

After over a decade running SCOTTeVEST, we were a thriving business. I certainly didn't need any partners on that end, and I wasn't going to give up 5% of my pocket empire to appear on a TV show. I could buy commercial time during the show for less money than that.

But, the opportunity to give TEC a proper launch - the opportunity to put the concept behind my patented clothing innovation on display for the whole world - was not something I was going to let slip away. I was willing to give up 5% of TEC, and I did.

That's why you never heard me breathe the word "SCOTTeVEST" on *Shark Tank*. If I said it while the cameras were rolling - **even if they later edited it out before airing** - I would owe 5% of my company.

One slip of the tongue and it would be a multi-million dollar mistake... and they knew it.

It scared the shit out of me.

Shark Bait

The Sharks truly have no fore-knowledge of the people appearing on the show. They are very savvy individuals, though, and they have an intimate knowledge of how the rules work... both the on-screen rules, and the behind-the-scenes rules.

That's why I believe that The Sharks were intentionally 'baiting' me the entire time I was being filmed. The more I challenged them, the more they pushed back.

I went into the *Shark Tank* pitching TEC, and I had to carefully tiptoe around the brand name that I spent years successfully building. If I slipped once and either mentioned SCOTTeVEST or countered any of their offers for SCOTTeVEST, part of SCOTTeVEST would belong to Mark Burnett and the producers of *Shark Tank* automatically and forever.

Imagine how hard it is to talk about your job without mentioning the name of the company. If I had, it would have cost me millions and for no good reason.

On a podcast* it was blatantly stated by Mark Cuban that his only goal was to make me cry on air, and I am not one to back down from a challenge. (He didn't make me cry by the way... not even close.) I think he gave it a pretty good shot, though unsuccessful.

Ultimately, I didn't take any of their bait.

I walked away from the possibility of a deal with The Sharks when it became apparent that they were only interested in SCOTTeVEST, and based on a bargain basement valuation.

I still firmly believe in the value of patents and the value of TEC. With all this background to the story, combined with my incredible passion for my companies, you can see why things got heated in the *Shark Tank*.

One important thing they left on the cutting room floor is that at the end of filming I did shake hands with each of the Sharks - other than Robert Herjavec - and they all told me what an amazing job I did. Even Mark Cuban. Robert, however, refused to shake my hand, which has NEVER happened to me after all my years as a professional. I thought it was actually pretty childish.

I told him how I felt, turned and walked away. That is when you hear him telling *me* to "show some respect" as I am walking out the door at the end of the episode. It still doesn't ring true telling me to show respect when he refused to shake my hand after the others did so graciously.

How Did I Get On *Shark Tank*?

A lot of people imagine what it would be like to get on *Shark Tank*, and this is the most frequently asked question I hear (other

---

* www.scottevest.com/cuban

than how someone else can get on *Shark Tank*). This is a brief account about what the months leading up to the airing entailed:

It was the summer of 2011. SCOTTeVEST was up and running and the company was growing steadily, adding employees and products regularly. I felt like we had an opportunity to pursue TEC - the licensing subsidiary of SCOTTeVEST - which as you know had been my original intention while developing SCOTTeVEST as a retail brand.

As an entrepreneur, I already loved the show *Shark Tank*, so we started to pursue an appearance as an opportunity to grow TEC. It seemed like it could be a great way to quickly grow the name, the business, and to license TEC to most major apparel brands.

It Started With An Email

We had occasionally worked with a freelance PR agent named Dina White, and we knew that she had also worked with some people involved with *Shark Tank*. We certainly did not get preferential treatment, but we did get two things: the email address of someone at the production company to CC on our application, and an assurance that my application would at least be seen by one person and not lost in the shuffle. Sometimes, that's all you can get.

This application, like the rehearsals, went through many iterations...draft after draft, until I hit "send."

Everything Begins With… Paperwork

I heard back within minutes that they were at least generally interested, and any time you don't get a hard NO from the media, it could be a yes. Actually, sometimes no still means yes if you persist long enough.

There were a lot of hoops to jump through - even initially - and I had a phone interview with Rhett Bachner, a producer from the show.

The questions were pretty generic. He asked me about myself, about what experiences shaped me, and about how I got the original idea for the product. It went pretty well, and in my

146

typical fashion, I followed up with supporting materials and emails.

After what felt like five rounds of video submissions, Skype calls and many communications, we got to the point of the contract. That consisted of a mountain of paperwork that we had to submit. This was when I discovered the 5% clause, and we were maybe 6 weeks into the process. Honestly, we freaked out a little, and more than a little duped. It took some clarification from the producers to ensure us that presenting TEC was not going to jeopardize 5% of SCOTTeVEST. This part was non-negotiable, and they put the risk of making a mistake squarely on my shoulders. It was worth the risk.

I found out that I was a semifinalist for the next season's episodes in mid-June, which meant the second round of forms and a video submission would be due about a month later. That's when I went into training.

Practice Makes Perfect

My team and I got to work scripting everything I had to say (the initial pitch to them) and all sorts of questions and answers that they might throw at me.

I also started my diet. Whenever filming was going to start, I was determined to look good, feel good and feel like I look good. Every camera puts ten pounds on me, so I dove right into what I called "the Ambien diet." I'd take a prescription sleep pill every night before I had the urge to snack after dinner. It's the only thing that works for me.

I worked with my team and with Rhett the producer on my pitch for TEC. We live-streamed rehearsals. That way I could get input from contractors who weren't on site in Sun Valley, and I filmed many variations and versions. Everyone was subject to strong confidentiality agreements. Part of the application and approval process is to submit videos to *Shark Tank* so they can judge how you come across on video, and also so they can give you some feedback on refining your pitch.

All in, I spent hundreds of hours practicing for *Shark Tank*. I was confident I could answer any question they could ask, but I was terrified about forgetting my pitch... or worse... saying

"SCOTTeVEST." For a shameless promoter, staying silent about the company I built for years was going to be incredibly difficult.

Patience Is Not My Virtue

Filming was originally supposed to take place in July in Los Angeles, but they added me to the September filming group instead. I took the time to continue training and continue losing weight. I went over the pitch again and again, and practiced loading and unloading my vest. (As I said, they didn't even show that part of my pitch in the final cut.)

I've already written about how intense the filming was. It was very hot and nerve-racking.* I was just afraid I would look like a sweaty mess.

Immediately after exiting The Tank, I was ushered into a mandatory meeting with the show's shrink. The visit had nothing to do with the content of my filming, but it was part of their process to make sure that the guests didn't wind up too scarred by the experience, and that they understood that contractually, their episode might not ever make it to air.

"Wait… did you see my taping?" The Shark Shrink nodded yes. "What are the odds that it won't air?"

The Shark Shrink looked left and looked right before leaning in and saying in a hushed tone, "Off the record - very, very, totally off the record - it would take a declaration of war for it not to air."

Just as I expected.

And immediately after that… more waiting. And more waiting. In the following months, I kept playing the filming experience over and over again in my head. I couldn't tell anyone about what happened in the Tank, but I'm transparent enough that most of my employees had some clue. Secrecy is not my forte, but I stuck to my *Shark Tank* contract: no one knew the outcome.

---

* I did a whole video interview about my experience if you want to hear all the gory details: www.scottevest.com/sharktank

The biggest secret of all was being kept from me as the months rolled on: I had no idea what would make it to screen.

In the Tank

We didn't know if or when my episode would air until the end of the year, and they didn't tell us the actual air date until two weeks before. Usually, we're fine with doing things "off the cuff" at SCOTTeVEST, but there were a lot of opportunities riding on *Shark Tank*, not the least of which was the millions of dollars of extra inventory we bought to be ready for the *Shark Tank* demand. As soon as we heard the air date, we jumped into action.

We had already mapped out how we would prepare for the episode and how we would react when it aired. At the time, I was the only one who knew the outcome, and none of us knew what the edit would be like. Of course, since there were no six-figure checks sent to us from a new billionaire supporter, I think most of my staff was able to piece together the broad strokes of what happened in the tank.

Two weeks of site updates, contingency plans, phone tests, staffing schedules, and press release writing followed. Customer Service staffed up and prepared for what would be an intensely busy night and a busy weekend. Most of the team was scheduled through the weekend, and we had backups in place in case they were swamped.

The marketing team focused on getting the website ready and on making sure people could find us when they went looking online. We bought AdWords keywords around every conceivable search term (Scott, Shark Tank, TEC, tech vest, shark tank vest, the jerk on shark tank, etc.) and set up redirects to funnel people from www.TechnologyEnabledClothing.com to a special landing page on the main SCOTTeVEST site. We were going to make some sales!

We anticipated having some press calls to deal with in the following days, and did everything possible to prep for the chaos we knew would follow.

On the night of the show, most of the marketing team came to my house to watch the episode at its first air time (East Coast time zone). The ET and PT time zones have the largest audiences, so there would be no warm up to the main event. We were going in hot. As nervous as I was in the filming process, I was even more nervous the night of the show. We filmed my reactions watching that first airing.*

The site did go down temporarily due to traffic, though we had been promised that we wouldn't have an issue. Compared to the thousands of orders I expected, we didn't get ANY orders. Something like 30 total for the whole night. That's like a slow Tuesday morning.

We had a large team in the office nonetheless, monitoring the site, answering calls, and preparing for post-TV press. I received thousands of emails about the show, and it was split about 50/50 between congratulations and vitriolic hate-mail. A fan once referred to me as "amicably abrasive" and it seemed that just like the camera adds 10 pounds to your appearance, my personality was likewise amplified.

The Aftermath

While my appearance on *Shark Tank* didn't do anything for sales, it did generate quite a bit of buzz. Some people lauded me for standing up to them and for keeping my head on my shoulders. But it would take more than congratulations to sell through all the extra inventory we purchased.

Other people blew me a lot of shit, saying that it was all a publicity stunt, that I was disrespectful, and a "patent troll." The press got in on the action, too, and I was covered in the "official" *Shark Tank* blog, *Forbes*, *Yahoo Voices*, *The Huffington Post* and Leo Laporte's *This Week in Technology*, among others. *The Huff Post* article is actually one of my favorite SCOTTeVEST articles of all time (see it at www.scottevest.com/STHuff).

---

* www.scottevest.com/sharktank

I issued a slightly different version of this statement on SCOTTeVEST.com to set the record straight....

Shark Tank Confessional

On Friday, March 2, I appeared on ABC's reality show *Shark Tank*. The premise of the show is as follows: an entrepreneur enters "the tank" with an idea and an offer. He or she pitches the product or business, and the decide whether or not they want to invest – the two parties either reach an agreement, or the entrepreneurs leave with nothing but some good exposure and a memorable experience.

Since the show aired on Friday, I have received overwhelming feedback from all over the board. The criticisms of those who took issue with the appearance fall into a few distinct categories. There are those who feel I used the platform merely for PR purposes – that I was never interested in a deal, but rather that I took advantage of the exposure. I am also receiving criticisms in regard to my demeanor – that I was disrespectful, aggressive, and less-than-cordial in my interactions with the (although usually expressed in more colorful terms).

My response is as follows: I entered the tank in hopes of gaining a strategic business partner who would help me establish my licensing company, TEC-Technology Enabled Clothing®, in a way that I have as yet been unable to do. The exposure inherent in an appearance on national television is something no entrepreneur would ignore. It was only after it became apparent that none of the Sharks were interested in making a deal for TEC that I decided to focus on the PR value of the experience.

I knew that although I did not get a deal with one of the Sharks, there would still be an opportunity to expose the world to TEC and to SCOTTeVEST, and I was not about to let that opportunity slip by. That said, there was no "free" publicity. As quoted at the end of the show: "Sony Pictures Television, a Designee of Mark Burnett, and ABC may receive equity in or a share of revenues generated by the businesses included in this program." I went in pitching TEC.

If I made a deal for SCOTTeVEST (or even mentioned the name), this company would also be subject to this agreement. Far from free publicity. Those who know me know that I am transparent to a fault; I cannot lie and I cannot act. What you saw was the real deal.

Publicity issue aside, I feel that the segment the public saw on Friday needs some context; there was a lot the public did not see from the interaction. The 60 minutes that I was in the tank was edited down to around 20. ABC, in the end, is trying to make good TV, and no one

151

can blame them for doing that job well (which begs the question, wasn't this a publicity stunt for them?). Granted, that is not the whole story, and to blame editing entirely would be a cop-out. What you saw were my honest reactions in the midst of a heated debate. I really did call Robert's initial offer insane, and I did tell Robert and Kevin they were out. I argued fiercely with Mark Cuban about intellectual property rights (he later indicated in a podcast that he made it his mission to make me cry), about standing by my patent and about the essential "American-ness" of the patent system.

But let's put this in perspective. How many times have you seen entrepreneurs – people who are really starting out, who have a great idea and need guidance and money – flounder into the tank and get taken advantage of? The difference between my segment and most others is that I am a businessman and that I was willing and able to engage the Sharks in a serious business interaction. I most definitely wanted to strike a deal with one or more of them, to get TEC off the ground as a licensing company with much more to offer than a single patent for a wire management system. But I was not about to turn wobbly kneed, forget why I was there, and sell away part of the company that my wife and I have put our hearts and souls into for over ten years.

Every time I watch the episode (which is not as many times as some people would like to believe), I see something else – I remember what happened to induce a reaction, or I think about what one of the Sharks said that set me off. I see the moments in which I appear arrogant, and knowing myself, I see what I really was: cornered. A good friend of mine wrote after he watched the show: "[you] come across as a guy who just loves his company and product..." I am a guy who loves his company and his product, and in those moments, I was a guy who saw that company threatened. Those Sharks are persuasive personalities, and they are powerful people. From a businessman's perspective, these are the people we look up to. The pressures add up – the intimidation factor, the thrill of being in the company of the Sharks – but as the Sharks and the rest of America learned, I would not be bullied into taking a bad deal.

To recap: I entered the tank with a deal that I thought was reasonable. I would like to mention that over the course of the weekend I have had interest in TEC alone, which confirms that this was a realistic pitch. The Sharks wanted something else, however. What ensued was an aggressive negotiation between equals, and we ended up not making a deal – it is that simple. No one on that panel is involved in the future of TEC or SCOTTeVEST, but I am confident that the future is bright for both. I want to thank my friends and followers for their support via Twitter, Facebook, and blogging; SCOTTeVEST was built on transparency and through direct relationships with customers. I want to emphasize that this is not "just TV" at this point. The issues that arose during the filming – about protecting intellectual property, about the value of my licensing subsidiary, and about what it means to negotiate in business – are very serious to me. Expect these debates to continue.

Scott Jordan
CEO & Founder of SCOTTeVEST

Did You Only Go On *Shark Tank* to Promote Yourself?

This is the question that I am most often asked about my experience on *Shark Tank*. The answer?...

You bet your ass I did, but I also wanted a deal and access to the Sharks contacts and resources. So... I guess I did not only go on *Shark Tank* to promote myself, but it was 90% of the reason I did. I really did want to make a deal for TEC, and I'm too transparent to lie about that.

Even though we didn't reach a deal, I do think it was successful. I suppose it matters on how you measure success. People recognize me when I go to trade shows, and it's been a great conversation starter... but you can't take that to the bank.

After *Shark Tank* aired, I definitely basked in the notoriety and played it for all it was worth. The appearance was not without its challenges, though.

I regret buying all the extra inventory leading up to it, but we have been able to sell down to a normal level of inventory by now (a few years later). I regret preparing as much as I did with the expectation that the immediate sales would be so dramatic. Those hundreds of hours could have been better spent. I also regret not suggesting that SCOTTeVEST could guarantee $100K in revenue to TEC each year, taking all the risk out of the Sharks getting repaid on their investments. It just didn't occur to me when I was in the tank.

Embracing the controversy and gaining press based on it has been the greatest payoff from *Shark Tank*.

P.S. *Shark Tank...*

While we're stirring up controversy, let me tell you some things about Mark Cuban.

A few times since the airing of *Shark Tank*, he's started some Twitter battles with me, primarily on the topic of patents. Honestly, I couldn't care less what he has to say most of the time, but when he directs his attention at me, I need to respond.

The main point of contention is a company based in the UK called ██████████. This is my book, and I'm not going to give them any more attention by naming them here, but you can figure it out if you really care. They blatantly knock off SCOTTeVEST products. And I mean blatantly.

If you put one of their vests next to ours and cover the logos, you literally cannot tell them apart. They even had me fooled until I tried to open a pocket and discovered how cheaply they were constructed.

Imitation is flattery, but copying is theft. My first thought was that I had to sue them, especially after I found out that the owner of the UK company had bought one of our vests months before his came out. It copied every detail of our vests (even the things we had planned to improve for the next version) and violated our patent.

It really pissed me off that the language on their site was all about how much time they spent developing the concept. Competition is fine, but straight-up copying is bullshit. Copying a patent is a violation.

Of course, some of this is public. And that's when Mark Cuban jumps in. He literally and in a public forum (Twitter) offers to pay the offending company's legal fees against me! I'm not making this up; see the exchange at www.scottevest.com/cubantwittercrisis.

It was bullshit, and I'm convinced it's what put the other company on the map. I'm just going to ignore them, and let them destroy themselves. I have no desire to become the Goliath so someone else can be David against me. This is one controversy that won't be embraced against me.

As for Mark Cuban, I think he's a billionaire bully who was incredibly lucky, and now he's sending the wrong message to anyone who would listen to him.

Enough said.

P.P.S. *Shark Tank*

I'm sure the *Shark Tank* lawyers are reviewing this chapter now. Bring it on!

CHAPTER 5
Engaging with Influencers

I've said it before, and I'll say it again: passion is the key ingredient to any entrepreneur's success. In fact, you can get away with a lot more if you are passionate about something, even if you are actually wrong.

Look at all the dynamic CEOs of tech startups that receive millions of dollars in VC money, round after eight-figure round, and have never turned a profit. Sure, there's power and appeal in the original idea, and there must be something in their projections, but what do you think sustains their investors' confidence? It's not referring back to the PowerPoint they saw three months ago. It's the passion of the team, and the communication of that passion.

How do you think Mark Cuban got so rich without his companies turning a profit? Ok, ok, I'm dropping it now....

Showing your passion for your company to other people does a funny thing. It draws them in and brings them along. Of course, some people are (much) better at this than others, and they often wind up being not only leaders, but influencers.

An influencer isn't necessarily someone in the traditional media, but that's where many of them do wind up. Social media is another place where influencers find their audience. There is a common thread between all influencers, regardless of the topic: they have immense amounts of passion and communicate it often. Sometimes without a word.

Anyone who experiences passion can recognize and appreciate it in others. If your passion overlaps with that of an influencer, they'll see it... they need to see it. That's just how passion works. And that's a golden opportunity to promote your passion.

One more thing about passionate people... they are usually passionate about more than one thing. Hap Klopp is the founder of The North Face, and a good friend. He is also the chairman of the SeV Advisory Board. He's passionate about the outdoor life, but also business and technology. When we first met, he recognized the passion I was capable of sharing, and we bonded on that basis.

Circa 2014

I often wondered what Hap saw in me, and I didn't really "get it" until I started to surround myself with other passionate people.

Nick Woodman, the CEO and founder of GoPro saw my passion when we met in Sun Valley, and I saw his. Same thing with Andy Dunn at Bonobos. It's electric and it's epic. I didn't always realize how powerful passion was or how to channel it, but I do now, and I'm still learning. It can be overwhelming to some people, but it's the most valuable commodity for any entrepreneurial company, and the CEO's highest and best use. How you communicate that passion is the most important part of the job.

Robert Scoble and Guy Kawasaki are both major influencers who reach millions of people with their passion for electronics, entrepreneurship and beyond. They also love SCOTTeVEST because it's more than just an article of clothing with lots of pockets... it embodies the passion and drive necessary to bring something great into the world.

I also count the Grammy®-winning Jazz visionary Herbie Hancock as a fan and a friend. He is as much of a gadget-lover as I am, and we connected when he bought some SeV items years ago. Since then, I've visited his home where we talked about music and technology and Buddhism for a few hours - all topics that he is very passionate about. And it was even more cool than it sounds!

Circa 2013

Influential people are passionate people. Ignite their enthusiasm for you and your brand, and amazing things can follow.

Like Minds

Through the entire history of SCOTTeVEST, I've been able to meet influential people who are passionate about the same things I am. Sometimes, I sought them out, and other times, we were connected organically or accidentally. But that connection around shared passions has always paved the way.

If you are a passionate, personal promoter, you will find yourself in a lot of interviews with the media. Some will be boring. Some will be clearly about the reporter filling a space on a page with words, or rounding out the gap between two commercial breaks. Just because someone covers a topic doesn't necessarily mean they love it.

But when you engage in a conversation (note the words "engage" and "conversation") with a member of the media who really gets it, it's magical. It's even more magical when it happens on camera. There have been many times when I've really ignited the passions of someone in media, and it came through on camera.

This Week in Technology

The first time I met Leo Laporte of *This Week in Technology* aka *TWiT*, he was on *TechTV* with Patrick Norton. I had been going to COMDEX, CTIA and CES (all shows related to the consumer electronics industry), and meeting many bloggers and reporters. At first look, it could be hard to tell who is a big shot and whose audience consisted entirely of their mom and their cat.

I didn't know anything about Leo, but I immediately liked him and we stayed in touch. It turned out that over time, a couple million other people liked him, too. Now he and his *TWiT* empire have their own podcast network and are one of the most influential tech media outlets.

I've been on Leo's show many times, and the conversations are always high energy. There is generally a live version of his show, and then a condensed, taped version that is published as a podcast. Anyone can tune in to the streamed version (and many do), and the conversation flows through the commercial breaks.

We care about the same things and have opinions about the same things, even if we disagree. That's how passion works, and it comes across on camera.* It's a long clip, but there are some great interactions in there.

Over the years, he's bought stuff and I've sent him stuff. All of his staff has at least some SCOTTeVEST gear, and most of them wear it all the time. Lots of TV, stage and film crews love our clothing because it's functional for them, durable and looks good,

---

* See for yourself at www.scottevest.com/leointerview

too. I don't remember ever seeing a podcast with Leo where he **wasn't** wearing something from my company.

But why?

It's not because I sent him some free shirts and jackets with his logo embroidered on it. It's not because he was trying to make some fashionista style statement. There are plenty of clothing lines out there that "check the boxes":

- Looks good and fits well
- Functional
- Good price, etc.

SCOTTeVEST does all that and more, but so what! Hundreds of other brands check those boxes, too. Leo wears SCOTTeVEST because the passions that drive him - technology, gadgets, clever attention to detail - are the same passions that drive SCOTTeVEST. It's not a nameless, faceless brand. Influencers are moved by things they feel a connection to, just like most people. We speak the same language, and when you get us talking, it's hard to get us to stop.

It's even hard to get him to stop talking about SCOTTeVEST when I'm NOT there. Get two passionate gadget fans together with a camera rolling and throw in the topic of SCOTTeVEST, and you're in for a show. Don't believe me? Watch this 9 minute clip of Leo and The Giz Wiz Dick DeBartolo (another gadget addict I've know for over a decade) going on and on about one of my jackets: www.scottevest.com/leovid.

What's the Big Idea?

There was a great interview show on CNBC called *The Big Idea with Donny Deutsch*. Donny is chairman of one of the world's most innovative and best known ad agencies, Deutsch, Inc. They've come up with commercials and campaigns that everyone remembers, and they are still considered to be among the most creative agencies.

Donny is a very influential guy. His show was on the air for a few years, and always got solid ratings because it gave the entrepreneurs' stories behind their brands. Guests on the show were entrepreneurs who had "the big ideas" and went on to turn those ideas in success. It was a fantastic show, and what really set it apart was how passionate its guests were.

Of course I wanted to be on it. Well, me and everyone else. I wrote them emails, I called them, I reached out through contacts for a few years. Nothing.

Then, one day out of the blue, I got a call from the producers of the show. They had seen an article about me and SCOTTeVEST and they wanted me on the show. I asked if my multi-year campaign to get on the show had finally worn them down, and they had no idea what I was talking about. It proved to me that getting press is the best way to get on TV. You just need to have enough stories to tell to keep them interested.

I flew to New York for the taping, and had a great time. I met Donny on-air, so when I unloaded all my pockets, his reactions were genuine. I pulled out a camera, a GPS device, a book, an iPod, a Blackberry, a magazine, travel documents, sunglasses, a

Camelbak water bladder and I showed off the patented Personal Area Network, too.

At one point, Donny said, "You really could blow this up... this thing could be hundreds of millions of dollars!"

I was for the first time on a major TV show able to give the demo I had given hundreds of times before. It was essentially the same demo I would give years later on *Shark Tank*, but on *The Big Idea* it wasn't left on the cutting room floor. Donny got it, and not only saw the potential of the idea, but was able to understand and communicate why it was successful.

My enthusiasm fed his enthusiasm and vice versa, and by the end we were on fire! Better yet, that passion came through to the audience. It was a massive opportunity for SCOTTeVEST, and that single TV appearance generated more sales than any other TV appearance, even though the audience couldn't have been more than a few hundred thousand people.

Herbie Hancock saw the episode and that's how he found us. Many other influencers I've met over the years watched that show, too. Passionate people like to see people being passionate.

I was invited back to be on the show again a couple months later leading up to CES (the Consumer Electronics Show) to be on a panel with other experts, including Tim Ferriss. Donny really liked my energy on the show, and I thought it was a good opportunity. I was glad I committed to losing 25 pounds after seeing myself on the show the first time.

Initially, I hadn't even planned on going to CES, but I figured I should change my plans since I would be talking about it.... No real product demo the second time, and it seemed like the energy wasn't as good as my first appearance. That can happen when you're on a panel and feel like you can't get in a word. But, I still wanted and needed to do it.

You can't build momentum if you stop after your first victory.

Know Your Customers

It's a business cliché to say "know your customers," but when I say it, I mean to **literally** know your customers. At least know their names. It doesn't matter if you are a small business or a large business... some of your best opportunities will slip by you if you don't know your customers. Any customer can be an influencer, and you might not even realize it.

I use the analogy of being like a neighborhood butcher shop. My customers come in and I learn their names, what they like, what they need, and do what I can to serve them better over time. At SCOTTeVEST, there is someone who looks at every order. That someone is my wife Laura.

Laura scans through every order and flags people for me to reach out to. She's noticed influencers and celebrities such as Amy Tan, Herbie Hancock and Woz this way. She's flagged media members including Greta Van Susteren, and Greta and I have been in touch now for a few years. Sometimes, we even see competitors ordering items. Hint: if you're going to spy on us and don't want us to know about it, don't have it delivered to your corporate office.

Laura's mind works like a machine, so over time she has been able to pick up on trends, identify the best customers by name and even get to know them a bit when there has been some interaction. I've spoken to quite a few fans on the phone or through Skype, and I'm convinced that this level of attention and caring is what makes our fan events not only successful and well-attended, but fun.

Part of knowing your customers is also caring what they think about your products. In the earlier days of SCOTTeVEST, I would follow up individually with customers. Now, we've reached a volume of sales where we need to automate that process, but my email address is on each follow-up. I want to know what they think.

When it comes to media samples, I would usually follow up immediately after the delivery tracking was updated. Contextual responses are powerful. I love to hear someone's first reaction when the package is delivered, and I've witnessed more than a few unboxings by influencers. I love immediacy, and I love honest first reactions. That's a great way to get to know someone.

While you're getting to know your customers, they're also getting to know you, too. Michael Mann (the director of *Heat, Ali, Collateral* and *Miami Vice*, both the TV show and the film) was a good customer when we first moved to Sun Valley. He had loved our 3.0 System - which was a multi-pocketed fleece jacket and an outer shell - and called me up one Sunday to ask about getting them as crew gifts.

Honestly, I didn't know how big he was, but I was happy to help him. He still reaches out every so often when he's working on a film and orders SCOTTeVESTs as gifts for his movie crew, friends and family.

Whatever you sell, you will probably have famous, influential fans at some point. How many restaurants, diners, and delis have you been in where there are signed photos of celebs on the walls? By all means, use this to your advantage as appropriately as possible... just don't be a douche about it.

Just remember, no one likes a liar.

Maybe I'm fortunate, but I'm not capable of lying. I'm a bad actor. I barely have any filters. And growing up in an environment where so much of what I was told was untrue, I have no tolerance for lies. I'm totally transparent, even when it's not in my best interest. I'm WYSIWYG (What You See Is What You Get), for better or for worse.

When I deal with an influencer, I keep their confidences. When I send out a press release to a reporter under embargo - meaning, it can't be published until a specific date and time - I expect them to honor the agreement. Sometimes it can be fun to play with things that are "off the record." In a conversation with a professional reporter, it's like a cone of silence drops down around that part of the discussion in an almost magical way. That can be fun, and doing that from time to time can build trust between you and a reporter.

When I become personally close to an influencer, I am hyper-aware of the limitations and boundaries of our friendship. I treat people - regardless of how influential or famous they are - like real people, and I don't use them. Anyone can be in awe of a celeb, but seriously, they're just people too. Be yourself.

Connections with influencers aren't and can't be all about the money. A friend of mine - Thomas Hawk - is an insanely well-known and well-respected photographer. He's as passionate about it as I am about SCOTTeVEST, and our careers overlap in many ways. He's done some amazing photo shoots with me, and he does it because he loves photography and respects me. He knows it's not about ROI.

Every Fan Can Be An Influencer, Too

If you are being asked to send $1,000 in samples to someone, yeah, you need to see how influential they are with hard numbers. Subscribers, viewers, fans, followers... something. But there are many influential people out there who you've never heard about. These subtle networks that spider out from certain people form the foundation of social media, and if you're not engaging people with it, you're not a passionate promoter.

When I first started SCOTTeVEST and only had a couple samples, I needed to find a way to get photographs of people wearing my products. Of course, since they were on pre-order, this was pretty tough. That's when I came up with the idea of the VESTibule of Fame and VESTimonials. (Did you really think I would be above making some terrible puns?)

Every time I would go to an event, a trade show or even a walk around the block, I would wear my eVEST 1.0 and bring a camera. I was showing off my invention constantly, and if the person I was speaking with was in the 50% who "got it" and didn't try to spray me with Mace, I would offer to let them try on the vest.

When they did, I would ask if I could take their picture wearing it for my site, and they almost always said yes. I wrote down their email address and name, and sent them a copy of the photo minutes later. I posted it to the SCOTTeVEST site along with their comments aka testimonials aka Vestimonials, and those hundreds of photos formed the VESTibule of Fame.

I even awarded "points" to customers for forwarding their photos, my newsletters and other referrals to their friends, and would have a drawing each month with a chance awarded for each point. It operated a little like an ethical pyramid scheme because the first people to participate got extra chances to win based on the number of people they referred, down through several generations of referrals. It was a pretty advanced social media sharing platform before such a thing really existed in the mainstream.

I also engaged customers by including their pictures as Vestimonial cards in my physical products from the very beginning. Drawing connections between fans and products in a real, physical way through photographs was a powerful component to the buzz around SCOTTeVEST. We still include Vestimonial cards, and we update them frequently. The Vestimonials and our other pocket cards were even discussed for uniqueness in Rohit Bhargava's best selling book *Personality Not Included*.

Over the years, I've met and interacted with some "super fans," or in some cases, just fans who have liked our product for a long time. Getting to know them through social media is fun, and the relationship sometimes goes beyond just occasional comments on Facebook. Sometimes we butt heads, but the goal is to be authentic in all contexts, so that's OK. Jorge Pereira and Dave Ciccone are two fellow gadget lovers and SCOTTeVEST fans who fit that mold.

I was and am convinced that if SCOTTeVEST could get our fans on our side, they would help promote us to their friends. A few years ago, we even did an all-fan catalog. We requested travel photos of people wearing SCOTTeVEST from everyone on our email list, and only used fan-submitted pictures in a 32 page, full-size catalog. This catalog was sent to everyone on our mailing list and was included with every product purchased for about a year.

We received some feedback on social media that we were being cheap by not hiring models, but in all seriousness, it cost a lot more to use the fan pics. We received THOUSANDS of photos. Some were of amazingly professional quality, but most needed a lot of work. Fans loved it. We wanted to engage our customers and put **their** face on our brand, and we succeeded.

The Ultimate Fan: Woz

Just like the interfaces on the first Apple computers he designed and built, Steve Wozniak aka Woz is WYSIWYG as in "What You See Is What You Get." If he likes something, he says it. If he doesn't like something, he says it. He does all the things he believes in with a humble, nonchalant enthusiasm that can be surprising. And - as far as I can tell - his core is made up of learning, teaching, kindness, cleverness and the pursuit of fun.

If there is a Zen icon of cool in my world, it's Woz. I'm happy and lucky to call him a friend.

I first met Woz after he bought something from SCOTTeVEST years ago. Knowing that he was a customer is directly due to knowing who our customers are. Laura spotted his name, and reaching out to him was something I couldn't pass up. I had been an Apple fanboy since I was a boy, or at least boy-ish. My first computer was an Apple IIc, and once the world of the iPod and iTunes opened up, I had no need to ever use a PC again.

It really felt like I made it when I knew that Woz had some of my creations. He was like the Pope, President and rock star of technology all rolled into one. I had to email him, and in my world, there is an incredibly short gap to jump between having to do something and actually doing it.

I sent him a brief note, telling him I was a big fan and was really happy he was a customer, and that I hoped he liked the products. I expected a response, but I thought it might be a one or two word reply and come through his assistant three weeks later.

The reply I received about four minutes later blew my mind: "The SeV is the perfect accessory for an iPod."

Woz was a fan... of me. Incredible.

Woz the Advisor

Through subsequent emails, I asked Woz to join the advisory board, and he accepted. In some ways, it felt like the ultimate validation. I was no longer just a gadget guy selling clothing. Woz recognized all the deeper purposes and value of SCOTTeVEST in the same way that I did. It was awesome, and it felt revolutionary in my life.

From time to time I would send him questions for which I wanted his feedback, and he was always prompt, honest and thorough in his responses. I've already told the story of the iPod spoof and how Woz offered to be in it. Let me reiterate: not taking him up on his offer was one of the dumbest things I've ever done.

After my appearance on Donny Deutsch, Woz sent me an email, unprompted:

From: Steve Wozniak ████████████████████
Sent: Sunday, September 23, 2007 2:08 PM
To: sjordan@scottevest.com
Subject: Re: Fyi

Dear Scott,

I have to tell you how much I admire you, for your entrepreneur story as well as your products. I can't remember when I saw such a great interview. I speak about the Apple story but yours is much more relevant for all the budding entrepreneurs out there. Everywhere I go there are dozens or hundreds of hungry faces of people who would love to hear your story.

I am a true fan of yours and am going to send that video to my list. I can't tell you how proud I am just to know you!

Highest regards,

Woz
--

-- tv is wake zone

Holy. Shit. This is Steve Wozniak, co-founder of Apple, and he says nicer things about me than my own family ever did. Ok, that's not such a stretch considering my family, but you know what I mean.

I am proud to admit... I cried like a baby out of utter joy, and that joy lasted for days. Nothing else mattered.

I contemplated sending him a full, heartfelt response, but in my typical fashion I opted for speed vs. completeness. I asked him if I could use his email publicly and he said "sure" within about 20 seconds.

That message from Woz is the only email I have ever printed and had framed.

Second Bite at the Apple: Woz-i-sodes

One of the most important things I do every day is follow up. I look back at flagged email threads, "blue sky" projects in our Basecamp project management software and calendared events. I have a system for revisiting past topics, and while it drives my employees crazy sometimes, it's a major part of our success as a business.

One day, I revisited the iPod spoof and Woz' willingness to participate in it, and it sparked an idea: we should do more spoof videos, and this time, they should star Woz. This was the genesis of the idea that came to be known as Woz-i-sodes.

Things came together pretty quickly. Concepts flew back and forth. What should we spoof? James Bond? *The Matrix*? *Star Wars*? We wanted the vignettes to be fun to shoot, funny and have some sort of tech angle, and of course a connection back to SCOTTeVEST.

With not much more than what I just described here, I floated the idea by Woz. If he was unable or unwilling to do it, the entire concept would need to change.

Woz was not only willing to do it, but he thought it would be great fun. He was all in. He even had a few hours free one day a couple weeks later when he would be in L.A. This could not be more perfect.

Now all I had to do was put together every single detail of making this happen. Until Woz said "yes," this had just been an idea. Now it had to become an event.

The Shoot

The scramble leading up to the day of the shoot was pretty intense, but nothing we haven't done before. At least this time I had some employees and contractors to help me move things along. We pretty quickly found a shooter/editor who had some decent creative chops and local assets in L.A.

The weeks leading up to the shoot were filled with logistics meetings, scripting, planning and finding support crew. Woz would be the star and I would be the co-star. We also hired an actress who was versatile and attractive enough to pull off a "Bond girl" role and a straight role equally. All in all, the team seemed to be pretty good. If the shoot went as smoothly as the prep, we would be in business.

I flew to L.A. from Sun Valley the night before the shoot, and made my way across town to the address of the studio. I can't recall exactly where it was, but it felt like a weird part of the city. Not necessarily dangerous, but it wasn't Hollywood. That was fine since I was paying for it... but when you can't even recognize what language the signs over the convenience stores are written in, that's a pretty clear indication that you're an outsider.

The studio turned out to be more of a... dingy boxing gym. Not quite as bad as the one in *Rocky* (but close). It could clearly be used as the set of a low-budget, coming-of-age, cliché boxing movie about a kid from the streets who learns to box as a way to stay out of trouble and eventually makes it big. In fact, I could probably write the script for that off the top of my head.

Good thing we weren't actually going to be seeing any of the surroundings, since everything would be shot on a green screen.

After checking out the location, I went out front and saw Woz and his assistant cresting a hill on their Segways, zipping down the sidewalk toward me. It was pretty unreal, like a sunset scene from a Western played in reverse. And on Segways. In L.A. Ok, bad example, but it was pretty cool.

As Woz came to a stop with the flourish of an expert Segway rider, he hopped off, shook my hand and we hugged. There was a point when I realized I was hugging him too tight, and for a little too long. He was proudly wearing SCOTTeVEST head to toe. After years of fandom and emailing, this was our first time meeting in the flesh. In fact, all of our interactions had been through email up to this point, not even a phone call.

I was actually pretty nervous. Not to shoot, but just to meet him. I don't think he knew just how much of an influence he had on me. What I did not expect was the calming effect Woz has. He put me at ease and reminded me that we were there to have fun. We did.

The Woz-i-sodes

The premise of the Woz-i-sodes did not change from the original concept: we were going to spoof some movies and scenes within the context of SCOTTeVEST, fill in the blanks with stuff we made up on the spot, and have a blast doing it. Mission accomplished.

There was a lot of activity on the set with the director, shooters, steamers, grips, lighting people and actors. We barely had any scripting, but we knew which scenes we wanted to spoof:

- *Star Wars*: Woz was dressed in a black hoodie covering most of his face as "Dark Vader." He delivered his line, "Scott - I am your fatherrrrr's mailman's cousin's sister's friend..." as the camera cuts to me, missing a hand.

- *Matrix*: Woz slips into "bullet time" to avoid gadgets being slung at him in slow-mo.

- Woz loses all his stuff in our *Dude, Where's My Car?* spoof. Of course, he finds them all again in his SCOTTeVEST.

- Woz Bond had him face off against henchmen and save the day.

- And Woz also became a genie in a magic 8-ball, was an elusive Bigfoot hunted by Sarah Palin, had his gadgets stolen by a giant fish and was shown in a few other random situations.

We shot scene after scene on green screen so the backgrounds could be digitally added in later. Half the time (all the time?) we had no idea what we were doing, since everything seemed very abstract. We had faith that the director and crew had the plan, and Woz went along with every idea, no matter how absurd it seemed at the time. He's a much better sport than I am.

Watch the videos at: www.scottevest.com/wozplaylist

What's the Difference Between a Mac and a PC?

The shooting day was going to be about six hours long, and when we broke for lunch, I had hoped I could pull Woz away into a remote corner of the room and pick his brain for a while. After all, this was the first time we had met in person. I didn't expect what transpired next, but it made me respect him even more.

He sat down with everyone else - the crew, the director, the actors - everyone, and we all ate together. He was the whole reason we were there, but there wasn't a hint of him acting like "the talent." Absolutely genuine, WYSIWYG. I have never been as calm on a set - any set - as he was that day.

After lunch, there were people coming up to say hi to Woz, whether they were directly involved with the shoot or were just sort of... around. On some level, I engineered this whole event to get to work with Woz, and he was just as generous with his time with me as with everyone else. Then, something happened that I will never forget.

There was a janitor at the space who had been moving around the periphery, picking up some pieces of trash from lunch, and doing things like that. He looked like he could have been homeless, or he could have at least been very convincingly cast as homeless on TV.

"Excuse me, Mr. Woze-ni-ak. So, when you changed from Windows XP to Vista I hated it! I couldn't figure out how to use the computer. Why did you do that?"

I was only a few feet away at the time, and I froze. I felt embarrassed even just hearing the question. WTF?

Well, Woz didn't miss a beat. He didn't look annoyed or taken aback at all.

Over the next ten or fifteen minutes, I watched as Woz patiently and excitedly explained the difference between a Mac and a PC, how different operating systems work and why they evolve over time. There was not a shade of condescension in his voice, and he spoke in a way that was not only clear and informative, but pretty damn inspiring, too.

He didn't slam PCs at all. I remember thinking that this is what greatness looks like, even as I started to get concerned that our filming time was slipping away.

He treated that janitor like he was the most important person in the room, and he didn't do it to put on a show. It was just Woz, the janitor and me. I think at his core, Woz loves to teach, and he is incredibly good at it. I also think that he's a good human being.

After concluding shooting later that day, I did get my chance to sit and talk to Woz. There was an auditorium attached to the building, and we sat back in the seats and discussed life, business and beyond.*

The Footage

I was very eager to see the results of our shoot, and to share them with Woz. So much was to be done in post-editing that it

---

* If you would like to see our conversation, you can watch it at www.scottevest.com/woztalk

seemed OK when scenes felt disjointed during shooting. It would all come together in the editing suite. Allegedly.

While I think that a lot of what we created was ok, and some of it was good, it definitely could have been better. The production values were... ok. The visuals added in post were... alright. But there was a lot more potential in the raw materials we created than wound up in the final product.

That's when it hit me: what if we repackage the Woz-i-sodes as the raw material for a green screen video contest? Everyone with basic video editing programs can participate, and it would be awesome to see some other perspectives on making the most of this footage that Woz had given up a full day to create with me. I wanted a fun end product that was worthy of the time and attention invested. And so the green screen contest was born.

We provided all of the unedited footage along with various other assets as the raw materials for the contest. In the end, we received over a dozen entries that ranged from groan-worthy Cub Scout skits up to rather sophisticated and well-produced attempts. I'm pretty sure at least one of them was made while the editor was taking LSD.

As much as I thought the original cuts fell short, I think the contest entries redeemed the experience. We live-streamed the announcement of the contest winners, and one of the videos received over 80K views on YouTube the last time I checked.*

The entire Woz-i-sodes experience was one of the coolest and most unique events of my life.

Beyond the Screen

We've crossed paths several times since the Woz-i-sodes.

Every time - and I'm not exaggerating - every single time I see an image or a video clip of Woz, he's wearing SCOTTeVEST. Ok, other than when he wears a tux. Whenever a new iPhone comes

---

* You can watch the finalists at www.scottevest.com/wozfinals

out, you'll find him in line at the Apple store to get one… wearing SCOTTeVEST.

After he appeared on *Dancing with the Stars*, Woz was interviewed on the *Jimmy Kimmel Show*… wearing SCOTTeVEST.

While I do send him new stuff from time to time, he's under no obligation to wear it, let alone anywhere he might be photographed. He is truly a fan, and that means more to me than any level of influence he might have on people exposed to him. But… since I am a passionate, shameless, personal promoter, I can't say I mind.

A couple years ago when we were announcing a new product called the Tropiformer, I had an idea involving Woz. The Tropiformer was a mash-up jacket/vest. It was as lightweight as a product we sold called the TROPIcal with magnetically attached sleeves from another product called the TransFORMER, hence Tropiformer. The name was meant to be an internal name, but we didn't have anything better when it came time to print the hangtags, so it stuck.

I also knew that despite co-founding Apple, Woz was publicly on record as having said he was a fan of both the iPhone AND Android phones from competing companies. He would carry and use both for different purposes, and he would do it all in his SCOTTeVEST. So why not get some photographs?

Woz likes to "stir the pot" every once in awhile, and say and do things that are controversial. He was all for having his photo taken with an iPhone in one hand and an Android in the other. Due to tight schedules, I wasn't there for the photoshoot, but we worked with a photographer Woz liked and trusted, and we got some great shots in our (then) brand new product.

Circa April 2013

Someday, I vow to get a photo of Woz imitating that iconic Albert Einstein photo, wearing a SCOTTeVEST.

The Birthday Invitation

I was lucky enough to get an invitation to Woz' 60th surprise birthday party from his amazing wife Janet. If you ask anyone who knows me if I can keep a secret, they'll say NO! I'm just too transparent. It really is hard for me to keep secrets, particularly fun ones like this. But I did it, and Woz was truly surprised.

The party was in San Francisco, and I planned a trip around it. Amy Tan agreed to be my date for the night, and she wound up also being my camerawoman for the video blog post from the party.* Woz even makes an appearance in the video, but it's a little hard to hear him over the band.

After bouncing from conversation to conversation for most of the night, Amy turned to me and said that she thought she was

_____

* You can see it at www.scottevest.com/wozparty

probably only the third most notorious person there after Woz...
and me.

Circa August 2010

A few hundred of Woz' closest friends and associates were in
attendance, and when the microphone was taken live and people
began to tell Woz stories to the crowd, I had to get in on the
action. I told the story of the janitor at the Woz-i-sode filming day
and looked out at the crowd of people who already knew Woz,
and watched as they nodded along. It wasn't an uncommon thing
if you know Woz.*

Surprisingly few people came up to the mic to tell a Woz story,
but the subjects of their stories were remarkably consistent. After
my turn at the microphone, Woz came up to me to thank me,
perhaps a little sheepishly.

If I learned one thing from dozens of interactions that night,
it's that:

Woz has absolutely no one to impress, and that's why he impresses everyone.

---

* My speech is available at www.scottevest.com/wozspeech

Endless Generosity

Woz is SCOTTeVEST's ultimate fan, and I can say without hesitation that his inspiration and guidance have helped me to become a better entrepreneur and more importantly a better person. He's someone I want to be like. If I've learned anything from his example, it's that being humble is one feature of a great leader. It's something I'm working on.

Regardless of the economics, regardless of the day-to-day struggles, Woz lives a passionate life. He loves great code and great design. He told me he still has the original handwritten code for the first Mac operating system. He is as passionate about gadgets as I am, and he revels in the fact that people using gadgets today can be as passionate about them as he was creating them.

My most sincere thank you is owed to Woz, and certainly not just for being my lifeline call on *Shark Tank*. From freedom to fun, he is a constant inspiration, and I'm honored to count him as a fan of SCOTTeVEST and a friend.

Brands Can Be Influencers, Too

As I learned by playing doubles tennis with my wife, having a good partner can make all the difference between winning and losing. That's why I've chosen to team up with other brands from time to time. While the economic details of a "strategic partnership" can't be overlooked, from the promoter's angle, it's all about the audience… and expanding your own.

From the early days of SCOTTeVEST, I pursued relationships with companies doing cool, techie things that related in some way to clothing. It wasn't about making money directly from the deal; in fact, if nothing happened beyond getting press and using their influence to grow my audience, that would be enough.

Xybernaut* developed wearable computers in the early 2000s, and SCOTTeVEST was the best way to carry them. Eleksen created soft buttons that could be sewn into clothing and control devices, and the PAN was the perfect way to connect the two ends.

When we created the solar jacket, we didn't try to create our own solar panels... we found a company that already made them. In fact, you could even put our TEC licensing deals with VF Corp and other clothing manufacturers in this category... the money changing hands was nominal next to the exposure potential of working together.

While SCOTTeVEST is mainly a direct-to-consumer brand, we do sell our products in various travel stores around the US, in a few international stores and through select online retailers.

ThinkGeek is our largest online reseller, and we've been doing business with them for over a decade. While their super-geeky copywriting and product selection are appealing, what makes them successful on their own is also what makes us successful together: they speak the same language as their customers, and share the same passions. We love it when they bring us into the same conversation, and together we're a potent force.

We've even collaborated* on product launches, like the Tropiformer Jacket and we cross-reference each other in press releases and media mentions whenever appropriate. They love our products and we love their audience. It's a good fit.

The Clothes On Their Backs

When a brand chooses to provide their products to their employees with the company logo emblazoned on it, I take that as a pretty good sign that they like and respect our stuff. When Intel, Microsoft and Symantec (among many, many others) ordered hundreds of SCOTTeVESTs at a time, I let the world know through press releases and my big mouth. My favorite part of

---

* www.scottevest.com/xybernaut
* www.scottevest.com/TGJacket

working with those companies was that they sought us out, not the other way around.

In Sun Valley every year, there is something called the Allen & Company Conference. Allen & Company are wealth managers, and while their conference is not heavily publicized, it is attended by just about every billionaire in the U.S. Not kidding, Google it. And guess what? They buy SCOTTeVESTs for each attendee.

We've been featured in the Nike Museum (yes, Nike has their own museum). It's part of a yearly event where they show off brands they think are inspirational to them. Nike is inspired by SCOTTeVEST... pretty wild. We've been shown in Disney's EPCOT Center as part of an exhibit of clothing of the future.*

Anything you can do to engage with brands and foster a connection is always a step in the right direction.

Influential Names

Celebrity endorsements have been a part of the advertising playbook for centuries, but as a passionate promoter, I don't think of a celeb endorsement as the best go-to plan. Partnering with a celeb is a totally different story because it provides the opportunity to have a win-win situation, where one of the wins isn't defined solely by the money you pay them.

SCOTTeVEST has partnered with some great brands like Leo Laporte's *TWiT* on branded merchandise, and we've gone beyond that with Andrew Zimmern. Andrew is the host of Travel Channel's *Bizarre Foods* (and other shows), and we met in person at a travel trade show where he was doing a presentation.

He had been a fan of our products, and I was a fan of his show. Earlier this year we launched a special edition Andrew Zimmern Road Ready Travel Vest based on a product already in our line. It gives Andrew something new to talk about with his

---

* www.scottevest.com/innovations

fans, and it's a connection that our audience appreciates as well. Win-win, and it wasn't based on paying random actor X to show up, smile and say a few lines into the camera for a paycheck. It's an organic connection, and it feels as genuine as it actually is.

Circa 2013

We took things even further with the #1 *New York Times* bestselling author Brad Thor. Brad writes thriller novels, and we happened to meet at an event in Sun Valley. He knew about our products, and over the course of the next year, we developed the Brad Thor Alpha Jacket. It was a product development from scratch, which is very costly and can take a long time...

...but it was worth it! Brad helped secure some major media coverage and we engaged our audience. Together, the first run of jackets sold out in record time. Then the second. Then the third. If you can connect with a celeb or brand that has their own stable of influencers, and you can tap into their audience as well as your own, the sky is the limit.

If you have fans like Woz, Hap Klopp, Peter Shankman and several other public figures who are fans of SCOTTeVEST, be sure to invite them to be on your Advisory Board. The obligations on them are minimal, but if they care enough about your brand to advise you, then you should acknowledge them for it.

Vendors

Every company uses products or services from other companies. When those products or services consistently perform well, and you grow to enjoy working with them, why not tell the world? Likewise, if a vendor of yours is going through their own marketing and promotion efforts (as any company that wants to stay in business must do), why not have them write about you?

It can be a very easy way to get some added press and to be associated directly with other great brands.

We have been approached by Google a few times to be the subject of a *beta* test or a case study with them. The first time was to test a new display mechanism on the Google AdWords platform, and most recently we worked with the Google Chrome team on a whitepaper about a new feature they rolled out and wanted to test. Sometimes, being a guinea pig is a great way to get some additional brand exposure.

Even if you don't have a long-standing relationship with Google, you can still get in on the action. We run A/B tests on our site all the time to see how variation A performs against variation B. Why not work with one of your vendors on some A/B tests and write a press release together if it works? This type of real-world information gets written about all the time by online trade journals. Sometimes, exposure is exposure.

I try to be the go-to source for quotes with my top vendors, as well. When AdRoll needed a quote about the effectiveness of their service for a profile in *INC. Magazine*, I was happy to provide them both a glowing review and hard statistics. They deserved the praise, and they knew that whatever I said about them would further the perception of their brand. Thanks to AdRoll and their PR team, SCOTTeVEST got another major mention in *INC.* But AdRoll had to know they could rely on us to tell the right story. More about what they do - retargeting - in the next chapter.

I have a great relationship with Stella Service and some of their employees. They rate the performance of customer service teams for online businesses, and it's not just their job, but their passion. When SCOTTeVEST's CS team was rated extremely well by them, it opened a conversation. Since we're passionate about providing great service, we bonded, and go out of our way to mention each other wherever appropriate. The Stella Seal is on our site, and they have referenced us in articles for the *New York Times* and other places.

Leveraging your vendors efforts can be as simple as providing a quote and a photo, as we did as a testimonial for Live Chat Inc., who provides the best live chat service we've found. It can be pretty involved, too. We've produced videos for our A/B testing experts Frictionless Commerce, our quality control company HQTS and even for our e-commerce platform Miva.

Miva sent a crew out for a day to shoot around the office and interview me pretty extensively, and the video turned out amazingly well. We both promoted the hell out of that video* and got a lot of mileage from it. What made it an effective piece is that there are hard stats in it, not just compliments. It also helped that Miva was using the information in a case study that painted them in a better light than a competitor, one which we had worked with before.

Trust me, the NetSuite story could be a book unto itself. Don't go near it.

If you don't have vendors beating down your doors to get your endorsements, just ask them if you can provide a quote, sound byte, or stat for their use. It never hurts to have more brand friends influencing their audience on your behalf.

---

* Watch it at www.scottevest.com/mivavid

CHAPTER 6
The Last Chapter is the First Chapter

When someone gets a blackbelt in karate, it's not the end of their learning, it's just the beginning. When someone lands the job of their dreams, it's just the first step towards making those dreams real. And when a passionate promoter has a pretty good idea of how to push their brand out into the world in a way that is uniquely their own... well, it's time to stop talking about it and start doing it.

When I was just starting out, SCOTTeVEST was a blank slate. My public persona was just a blank slate, too. In fact, it wasn't until about 2007 or 2008 that many people outside the media realized that the name SCOTTeVEST wasn't just a cryptic, hard to remember brand name, but that there was actually a guy named Scott behind it. In case I didn't mention it, that Scott behind SCOTTeVEST was me.

Uhhh... just making sure you're paying attention.

As the world changes, even a passionate, personal promoter needs to be ready to change, too. It's like a caterpillar going into a cocoon to emerge as a butterfly, or a frozen Big Bomb Burrito entering the microwave to be transformed into a delicious, gut-busting treat.

Whether you're starting from a blank slate or starting over with a blank slate, reinvention is the tool in the passionate promoter's toolkit that lets you reboot... for fun and profit. I've done it many times to varying degrees.

It works.

Reinvent Your Message

So what do I mean by reinvention? Merriam Webster defines "reinvention" as....

Whoa whoa whoa whoa - stop right there. If you ever see anyone start a sentence with anything like that, leave immediately. You have my permission to slap them if possible.

Reinvention is pretty simple. Usually, reinvention is all spin. It's finding an angle and emphasizing it more than you emphasized that angle before.

It's not necessarily a 180 degree turn. It's the difference between saying "you can carry your gadgets with you," and "you can carry your gadgets with you while traveling." Reinvention doesn't need to alter the core of your message, just refine it. As long as you are speaking to a new audience, or a prompting a current audience with a new mindset, you are reinventing.

The Nine Lives of SCOTTeVEST

If you haven't been sleep-reading the entire book, you know I love gadgets and started SCOTTeVEST to be a better way of carrying them around. Even from the beginning of the company, we've sold them to all types of people: photographers, commuters, gadget-lovers, birders, concealed carriers and undercover police, travelers, special ops, doctors, bikers and everyone in between.

Over time we noticed that even though our market was broad, nine times out of ten when people would post photos of themselves on social media or email them to us, they were travel photos. It seems really obvious now, but a lot of our customers became customers in the first place because they were planning a trip, and having the world's best multi-pocket clothing makes perfect sense in that context.

Then, they would wear their SCOTTeVEST on their trip, and take photos while wearing it. $1 + 1 = 2$. It had been staring us in the face for a while, and it was time for a shift, a reinvention.

SCOTTeVEST would be a travel clothing company.

But we wouldn't just be any travel clothing company. We didn't want to cater only to people who spend 9 months of the year traversing the globe. We certainly didn't want to appeal only to people who dress like they're going on safari 365 days of the year (you know who you are).

SCOTTeVEST wasn't just going to be for your trip. It's for the trip of your life. Reinventing ourselves as a travel clothing company was the gateway into our customer's year-round experience. We knew that if someone tried the product under the heightened circumstances of a travel, they would see the value of our products for their everyday life when they got home.

Reinvention doesn't require changing everything. Just changing the hook.

After all, a butterfly is still a bug.

(Did I just disappoint all the romantics out there?)

Go to Extremes

A million other books and experts talk about finding your customer's pain points and addressing areas of friction, blah blah blah. If you are passionate about what you do, you already know where the pain points are. Magnify them and offer a solution.

When we shifted our messaging to speak to travelers head-on, a few things happened. We hit a nerve... sales went up. We had tons of new photos to reinforce our message. We had a new hook to bring people in the door.

But as we got deeper into what it means to travel, we uncovered even more new things:

- If you could carry your things in pockets vs. in a bag, the customer could save on baggage fees.

- Pockets allowed people to travel light... or travel heavy if they considered SeV to be a third carry-on.

- Airport security was a breeze when you could take off all your pockets at once and slide them through the x-ray instead of looking for that loose coin that keeps setting off the metal detector.

We knew we were really onto something when the deeper we scratched the surface, the more sub-messages, hooks and opportunities arose. As with the Delta "beat the system" ~~debacle~~ PR feeding frenzy, the more the airlines got pissed off at us, the better. The audience almost always sides with David, not Goliath.

The idea of getting pickpocketed is a scary thing, but it's impossible to pickpocket someone through two layers of zippers in their SCOTTeVEST. We put up a $1,000 Pickpocket Proof Challenge to replace the pocket contents of anyone pickpocketed wearing a SCOTTeVEST, and we've never had to make good on the guarantee.

We amplified the message of convenient travel. We created a product called the Carry-on Coat with 30-something massive pockets. It looked like a trench coat, but it could hold more things than a carry-on, including several outfits of clothes. It's not my favorite product, but it certainly solidified the message of how you can use a SCOTTeVEST.

We even created a campaign called the No Baggage Challenge, and later renamed the No Baggage Challenge for Charity. We worked with Rolf Potts, who is a world traveler and the author of *Vagabonding*, amongst other highly popular travel books. He traveled for six weeks through 12 countries across 5 continents with ONLY the clothes on his back and whatever he could carry in his SCOTTeVEST pockets.*

It wasn't nearly as un-hygienic as it sounds, since he comfortably able to pack everything, and the experience fit perfectly with his style of travel. Subsequent No Baggage Challenges followed, and they were each undertaken for a different charity. The longest was a 90 day trip across South America, but the No Baggage Challenges touched Haiti, Japan

---

* Read about it at www.scottevest.com/NBCRolf

and even spanned a 2,400 mile trek along India's most dangerous road in an auto-rickshaw.

They were not for the faint of heart, but they really embraced the concepts of adventure, daring and exploration that we wanted to associate with SCOTTeVEST. The charity component was vital. Many of the places visited by the No Baggage Challengers were poor, and the people living there may have had barely more than the clothes on their backs, and nothing in their pockets. Kiva.org was one of our charity partners for part of the campaign.

The Battlestar

There was a point not all that long ago when if you asked me who my market was, I would say, "everyone." In fact, I've said it a lot. Double in fact, it's true. But that doesn't exactly make the individual members of an audience feel special or like you're speaking to them as someone who's passionate about the same things they are.

"Segmentation" isn't exactly a sexy term, but that's what most marketers call the solution to this issue. At SCOTTeVEST, we call it "Battlestar," as in *Galactica*, as in the show. This is why...

Several years ago when the show was a current, pop-culture phenomenon, my wife Laura was still handling all the SCOTTeVEST customer service interactions. This was a big part of how we were able to "know our customers" for years. Through the course of her interactions, customers would sometimes get chatty, and more than a few times, they asked if she had seen the show *Battlestar Galactica*.

When she told them she hadn't seen the show, they would begin to gush about it. Their enthusiasm reminded her of the enthusiasm they expressed for our products. Definitely worth Googling. (I even blogged about it.*)

Nearly 9,000 results linking SCOTTeVEST and *Battlestar*? No way. I dug a little deeper, and it was true. There were lots of

---

* www.scottevest.com/bsg

191

crossovers between the interests of *BSG* fans and SeV fans, and it sparked an idea and a shorthand that we have used to describe our targeted marketing programs ever since: Battlestar.

For us, the term has many layers of meaning that go beyond what is considered one of the greatest sci-fi shows of all time. We use it as a code word to describe people who are interested in anything with a similar passion to how we feel for SCOTTeVEST.

Included in the list of Battlestar-ers are birders, photographers, motorcyclists, runners, fly fishermen, shooters, doctors, tour guides, geocachers, emergency medical personnel, fanny pack and money belt fans, dog walkers, concert and sporting event attendees, Trekkies and dozens and dozens of other interest groups.

There are so many groups that it's not possible to develop a specific product for each one, but we make it a point to speak to each group in language that makes sense for their interest, and shows that we "get it." For birders, we spoke with people who are passionate about birdwatching, collected a list of the things they actually carry, and created graphics to reflect how they would use our products. We went so far as to create graphics for comic book collectors and fans of various other TV shows with passionate, cult-like followings.

This is re-invention for a purpose, and not just because we thought we needed to shake things up, or because we felt bored. Everything we've done speaks to a specific group, but we make it a point not to alienate others. There is room for a lot of perspectives and a lot of passions.

Even if we're not passionate about the same things our customers are, I can appreciate their passion. They recognize mine, and that's part of the appeal of my brand to them. Putting the shoe in the other pocket (hey - I'm trying to start a new slang phrase here!) is the least we can do to engage their interest and show them that we respect what they love. This is what makes ThinkGeek such a special company and a special partner.

TV host Chris Hardwick might be thought of by some people as the king of nerds, and he summed it up beautifully on the *Jimmy Fallon Show* last year when he said:

"It's not what you like that makes someone a nerd, I think it's how intensely and passionately you like those things. A nerd superpower is to understand something more than any other living creature on the planet, and then shame them with that knowledge."

Reinvention falls flat without the passion to back it up.

Keeping Up with the Jetsons

As much as I consider our clothing designs to be classic and pretty close to timeless since we're never chasing fashion trends, there is one part of the gadget-loving SCOTTeVEST ethos that requires regular review: what people carry in their pockets.

The leap from AA-powered CD players to iPods was pretty steep. The favoring of touchscreen and "candybar" phones over flip phones was significant. And jumping into the world of tablets from… where?... magazines?... catalogs?... was a game changer when it came to the devices that many people carry with them on a daily basis.

For me, it was pretty easy to make sure that SCOTTeVEST's pockets carried the latest and greatest gadgets because those were the gadgets I had or wanted to have. But there were times when we had to reinvent either our messaging or our physical products to keep up with the times.

I mentioned before that our PadPocket™ (originally called the PubPocket™) was intended for magazines and books before the iPad was unleashed on the world. We didn't need to alter our clothing, but it gave us some critical dimensions to work with: all future SCOTTeVESTs had to be designed to accommodate an iPad, or it had to be clearly decided that a style would NOT hold an iPad. It gave us a language and a purpose around which to frame our purpose-driven clothing.

When iPods came out, I discovered that you could control them through the thin lining of some pockets, and that became a feature I could discuss. A few years later we discovered the clear touch material that now allows people to SEE and control their touchscreen phones without removing them from their pocket.

When phone sizes started to creep up to massive "phablet" proportions, we made sure to scale up our pockets a reasonable amount to accommodate them. If a pocket was too small for a particularly voluminous device, we made it clear and made sure our customer service agents had the info needed to answer questions authoritatively.

RFID tags are now in all U.S. passports and many credit cards. Too bad it's so easy for thieves to digitally pickpocket people by surreptitiously "skimming" the information from their important documents with a pocket-sized device. The solution? Find a material that could block the skimmers and line a pocket with it.

The patented Personal Area Network (PAN) works equally well routing headphone wires from a pocket to the collar as it does connecting a pocket to another pocket with a battery pack. When I first invented the eVEST 1.0, fuel cells and battery packs were huge, heavy and didn't last very long. Now, I can recharge my phone using a battery pack barely larger than my thumb.

With the battery longevity issues related to Google Glass, this was a perfect connection to make, and we reinvented SCOTTeVEST as the ultimate Google Glass accessory to keep it charged and running all day long. We even debuted it at CES by putting SCOTTeVESTs on the backs of some of the influencers actually using Glass at the show: Robert Scoble, Joel Comm, Chris Voss, Xavier Lanier and the *Gottabemobile.com* team, along with many other ambassadors.*

The ultimate gadget vest was reinvented as the core platform for the next generation of wearable computers. If augmented reality glasses are next, we'll be there. If wrist-top devices take off, we'll be there. If robotically enhanced limbs follow, guess who'll be supporting them? When wireless power becomes ubiquitous, SCOTTeVEST will have an angle.

---

* See the press release here www.scottevest.com/glass

Reinvention is about keeping up with the changes that affect the core of your business, and having the passion and imagination to go over, under, around or through roadblocks.

There are always hidden opportunities if you have a mindset of reinvention.

Align Your Biz and Life

I think about my business a lot. As in, constantly. All the time. My mind is always racing with ideas and searching for angles. I know I'm not alone in this... it comes with being passionate about a subject and throwing yourself into exploring it. Way down deep inside, I'm an intensely curious person, and I'm always trying to find or make connections between people, places and things. That's part of the entrepreneur bug.

So it should be no surprise that major parts of both my life and business have aligned in significant ways. In fact, the more your business and life align, the more promoting one will promote the other, and the more enjoying one will build your enjoyment of the other.

Moving to Sun Valley is, of course, my biggest example. Being a traveler and a gadget guy who realized that other people have the same inconveniences and problems that I did certainly qualifies as another example. Fan events when I happen to be traveling to a city fit in the example column, too. But it doesn't stop there. Not even close.

In July 2013, Laura and I embarked on a new adventure: reinventing the top floor of the SCOTTeVEST office building to become our home. With the help of a small army of contractors, we blew the roof off (literally) and tore everything down as much as structurally possible. It was cathartic to strip it to nothing and watch as our vision came together first as 3D renderings and then as physical reality.

Circa 2013, Mt. Baldy reflecting in windows of SeV HQ

The decision to live above our office was a pretty easy one. The building is in downtown Ketchum, ID (connected to Sun Valley). There is a spectacular view of Mt. Baldy; no exaggeration, it's probably the best unobstructed view in town. And because Laura's typical work day starts at 1 AM since she is an extreme morning person, I wanted to reduce her previous 4 minute commute to as few steps as possible. Now, it is literally steps. Perhaps she'll sleep in until 2AM now.

The same creative energy that drives SCOTTeVEST drove the creation of our home, so there are definitely parallels with the brand. Laura designed a bed with hidden "pockets" for all the stuff that we need to have by the bed, and we're thinking of expanding the SCOTTeVEST brand to sell it. The clean aesthetic of our products carries through to the no frills materials and layout of our home. And the end product represents an abstract vision made concrete. (Really... most of the surfaces are concrete.)

I could fill a book with all the connections between the design and creation of our home and the business. Maybe that will be the next one. But expect to see some major press about the process and the outcome.

I don't have what you would call a work-life balance. My work is my life and vice versa. It doesn't grate on me or wear me down the way having a "real job" did. I'm in charge of my own schedule, and every time I work it's because I choose to work. I just choose to work a lot, and I'm successful because of it.

Furthering the connection between Scott and SCOTTeVEST is my blowout 50th birthday party. As of this writing, it's about a month away, but I expect it to be epic. It will be the "unveiling" of our new home, and I've invited everyone. Friends, family, press contacts I've known for years and yes, I've even invited some customers. They're coming, too.

Who ever does stuff like that? That's part of the reason why I did it. I wanted to...

Make it personal.

The Ultimate Reinvention: Entrepreneur to Leader

It takes more than passion, promotion and money to **sustain** a business. It requires leadership and management (and a dozen other things, but let's just stick with these two for now).

Before I started SCOTTeVEST, I moved from working in a dysfunctional family business to working in law firms to working in a dysfunctional startup in one of the most wild west periods of modern American business. In other words, I had never worked for a "real" company. I had never been part of a typical business environment or dealt with employees.

This both helped me and hurt me.

I definitely had to learn things on the fly, but for every stumble and everything I should have known better than to do (but did anyway), I feel like my unique approach got me where I am today. I'm proud to be one of the biggest local employers in my area, and I'm proud that I keep factories hopping and UPS delivering packages all year long.

But a funny thing happened - and had to happen - as I went from being a one-man show to a business owner. I had to evolve as a person. I had to develop leadership skills, and rely on motivations other than money to get the best work out of my employees and contractors. I had to create a corporate culture for people to understand the core values that make SCOTTeVEST successful, so they can continue in the same vein when I'm not looking over their shoulders.

It was really tough. Being passionate and inspiring people comes naturally to me, but leadership continues after the pep talk ends. This was my hardest, most important reinvention ever.

What follows is a rough-and-ready overview of what my employees call "The Scott OS" as in "Operating System." During hiring interviews and contractor evaluations, the Scott OS is an important topic of conversation. It encapsulates the SCOTTeVEST corporate culture and all the important mindsets that keep the wheels on the SCOTTeVEST bus.

The Scott OS: Corporate Culture

You know me as a passionate, personal promoter, but here is a concentrated dose of how I approach **running** my business with the same philosophy and drive that I apply to promoting it. If you want to be successful, you can't have one without the other....

We define corporate culture as what we do consistently as individuals and as a group to further the goals of the organization. Bottom line: the mindset, expectations and requirements apply equally to everyone connected to the company. It is an all-or-nothing undertaking.

Honesty, Integrity, Transparency:

- Say what you do and do what you say. Period.

- Be honest - with us, each other and yourself. This is why we are always measuring back to metrics and numbers... they don't lie, even if we don't like the story they are telling us. We need to check back, follow-up, measure and improve on everything we do.

- If you make a mistake, own it - correct it, take accountability, and don't make it again. The people who have been at SeV the longest have already made most of the mistakes you can make... once. So learn from our mistakes.

Learn the phrase, "I'll Figure It Out":

- We expect you to figure things out on your own. When you ask a question, be sure to have exhausted all resources first.

- Don't throw your hands up at the first sign of resistance. Solving a difficult problem helps you build the tools to solve even bigger ones. There is always a solution.

Embrace the Implementer Mentality:

- What is an implementer? Someone who gets shit done!

- One of the highest compliments someone at SCOTTeVEST can pay you is to call you an implementer.

Speed, Accuracy, and Efficiency:

- Work with efficiency, urgency, speed, accuracy, and don't forget to laugh!

- Some things can be done "quick and dirty" and don't require pondering, ideating or careful planning. We are committed to rewarding people who can embrace moving fast without giving up accuracy.

- There's a difference between working hard and spinning wheels, so make sure your efforts are productive.

- Be a multi-tasker and learn to work efficiently in a high-demand, team oriented, and fast-paced environment.

- Remember the Santa Clause: Make lists and check them off. If you do this, communicate what is on your list, and if you complete your list items on time you will succeed 100% of the time.

No F---ing Drama:

- Have a positive attitude when cooperating with your co-workers. Communicate and be non-confrontational, but don't ever be afraid to push back.

- Most problems are not world-ending problems… they are a puzzle to solve.

- Be able to take criticism and show your ability to adapt to changes.

- Be courteous. Courtesy saves time and minimizes misunderstandings, but don't mistake brevity for anger. We all have a lot going on. We have had some customers for over a decade, and we actually KNOW them, and they know us. This comes from caring and being courteous.

- Work to your highest ability at all times. Sometimes things fall short, but it shouldn't ever be because we didn't do everything we can do to succeed.

Email Etiquette:

- ALWAYS "reply all" unless there is a reason not to do so.

- Reply quickly. In an organization that moves as fast as ours, an hour between responses is like a week. If you don't have time to reply immediately confirm receipt even if it's just "ok" or "got it" or "on my list for 10AM tomorrow," and be thorough in your responses or let others know that you need more time to send a thorough response.

- Be clear and concise and get your point across quickly rather than typing paragraphs. Do not be long-winded.

- Every email should move the topic of the email thread forward. Emails are tools of action, not conversation.

Respect Deadlines:

- If you have an action item and a deadline, you have agreed to a contract that you will get it done on time. EVERYONE in the organization is counting on you to do it. That may mean working through lunch, or coming in early or staying late, but little promises can snowball into big problems if they are not done.

- If you can't meet a deadline, communicate that you need more time BEFORE the last minute. Ask for extra time as soon as you know, NOT when it is supposed to be done. Provide the date/time when you can accomplish it.

- If you can't complete something immediately, at least keep it alive - it's like keeping multiple balloons in the air.

As important as it is for a corporate culture to be well-defined and documented, it's impossible to just spout out a bunch of bullet points and make them an organic part of people's mindsets and daily approach.

To support the importance of the SCOTTeVEST culture, we always have tech training available to use tools like Basecamp and Google Apps better, and we subscribe to Lynda.com for ongoing learning. Every Friday, the whole company comes together for Friday lunch and we sometimes Skype our key contractors with video feeds. That is our time to come together as a tribe and connect on a human level.

At the end of the day, this is my key sentiment to all employees and contractors: If you want more out of your job, make it happen. Be diplomatic about it and make it your dream job, or just leave.

Even though we've been in business since 2000, we are still a "new" company compared to the decades that exist ahead of us. I want every employee to know they are in control of their own careers.

My List of 5 Things I wish I knew when interviewing for SCOTTeVEST
by Marshall Rule, VP of Marketing and Operations

1. This job will enable me freedom. Freedom in scheduling my time, freedom in projects to work on...as long as people treat that freedom as a privilege.

2. Scott is intense and passionate. He is not angry. Listen to the actual words he says. If you get hung up on the tone in which he says it - you will not get the point.

3. It's okay to be wrong at SeV. Just know why you were wrong, what went wrong, and don't make the same mistake twice. The more transparent you are, the less you will be wrong (the more chances you will have to be corrected early on in the process).

4. If you make other people's jobs easier, you will be more valuable. Everyone here works hard - so the more we all keep each other's jobs in mind when doing things - the more we get done collectively. Don't do a project without knowing how it will affect other people.

5. The ability to move quickly and change plans on the fly is vital to success here.

Marshall's five points are now a guiding concept for what we want all employees to be able to achieve.

The Scott OS: Hiring

Hiring is one of the most difficult yet necessary things any business owner will face... and let's face it, I'm not the easiest person to work for. You need some level of help for growth, but as a business owner, employee problems are automatically your problems

- **Hire slowly:** Don't staff up until you feel the need for someone else to do the job, and know what that job entails. We use DiSC Profiles, HireSelect and other personality and aptitude tests to gauge how well someone can fit and work. Even with these tests there are no guarantees. But before any hiring is done, the candidate needs to meet and get a sign-off from all the key players in the organization.

- **No bozos:** There's this thing called a "bozo explosion" and Guy Kawasaki created the definitive blog post about it.* Without going into all the details of what a bozo explosion is - or the story of the one we survived - know this one piece of advice: be 100% sure that whoever you give the power of hiring other people is competent and careful at their job. The alternative is realizing that the last eight hires in your company had no business being hired, and you'll need to unwind the mess for the next two years. Enough said.

- **Fire fast:** This is not a popular sentiment, but I stand by it. If someone is not working out, and has been told what they need to do to keep their job, and is for whatever reason incapable or unwilling to do what is necessary, pull off the Band-Aid. They're not going to get any better over time, and having an unhappy, unproductive person in your organization can drag down everyone else. If they have been given a final warning, make sure it is truly a final warning. Have no doubt... this can get you a reputation.

The Scott OS: The importance of meaningful relationships

Whether they are customers, employees, press, vendors, suppliers or friends, there are many relationships worth building and maintaining that have nothing to do with a measurable ROI.

I've been working with the same contract graphic designer/developer - Robert Avedissian from Avetar.com - since 2006. Why? He does amazing work, and when I don't think something represents his best effort, I tell him. Then he makes it better and improves his process through our joint process. We challenge each other, and the investment we've made in each other pays off in the quality of work we can achieve together. He designed the cover for this book using photographs from Thomas Hawk.

---

* www.scottevest.com/bozo

After many years, we still work with Karen Jones at LSIdaho for our freight logistics and customs/import work. Karen and her team take great care of us. We still source many of our clothing styles through KT who did the very first eVEST 1.0 for the same reasons.

Until 2008, Laura or I (ok... mostly Laura) would pack and ship every single SCOTTeVEST order, and there was never a single shipping error in the entire time she did it. When we grew large enough to need a dedicated fulfillment center, we spent a lot of time and energy making sure we found a partner who had the same OCD level of precision we have. When we found the firm DTI outside of Chicago –- and specifically Tim and Dan, the owners – we made the move. They have been our shipping partners ever since, and their ability to ship things out quickly and accurately is part of what makes SCOTTeVEST tick.

We would be almost nowhere without the press. But you already know how important it is to build relationships with them. Don't take any relationships for granted. The right people - or even just one right person - can change everything for the future of your company.

The Scott OS: Micro-management isn't bad

Somehow, the idea of "micromanagement" has gotten a bad rap. I'm sure that it came from employees (or former employees) who felt that they were not trusted to do their jobs without supervision. But let me set something straight... micromanagement isn't a bad thing!

If given the choice between micromanagement and hands-off management, I'll pick the micro option ten times out of ten. If you look at all the people who has been accused of being a micromanager, you'll find that they have probably also been successful.

What some people think of as diva behavior in musicians and performers can sometimes boil down to a need for attention to detail. Van Halen's famous ban on brown M&Ms in their dressing room at concerts stemmed from such a need. If the venue could not follow a small request like that, how could they be trusted to ensure the stage pyrotechnics were safe and there was proper security?

In much the same way, I think micromanagement is necessary until an employee can prove time and time again that their level of self-management is comparable to your level of micromanagement. They need to demonstrate that the small details are covered so thoroughly that you don't need to worry about any of the details.

- **Steve Jobs** was a legendary micromanager. Uhh, I think it worked.

- **Hap Klopp**, founder of The North Face employs a 90/10 rule: assume you will need to bring a project 90% of the way, and "the other people" will bring it 10% of the way to completion. Maintain this assumption until you are consistently proven wrong; that's when you know you are working with a professional.

- **J.Crew's CEO Mickey Drexler** said in an interview with CNBC, "The world needs more micromanagers running companies today.... I love micromanagers. Why? Because I know they care about every customer."

I couldn't agree more. The only way to control your brand... is to control your brand. Your employees need to raise their personal standards to meet yours, and that means yours need to be higher than theirs and communicated clearly. Usually loudly, too. This doesn't mean angrily, but it's definitely the time to channel your passion into something inspirational.

There is a point in micromanagement where is loses its effectiveness. Don't cross the line, but make sure you go up to that line.

The Scott OS: Follow up

Imagine me talking like a gum-chomping, mall-visiting, hair-twirling, up-speaking "Valley Girl" for just a second: "following up and measuring back are like the freakin' most important things to do EVER." </valley_girl_voice_off>

It's true. You could literally be - and I mean this in the real way the word is used, not the way Millennials use it - the absolute BEST, most passionate promoter the world has ever known, and you will FAIL if you don't master the art of following up.

Likewise, you could be a little charismatic, fairly dynamic. and a pretty good promoter... but if you are an amazing follow-upper, you will WIN. It's the one easily learnable skill that can close the gap between what you are good at and what you can accomplish.

- **Email follow ups:** If you send an email or a note to press or to anyone who can affect the success of your company in any way, flag that note for a follow up a few days out. Recognize that not everyone is working on your time schedule. Recognize that there are two kinds of people - responsive people and unresponsive people. And recognize that if you want to get shit done, it doesn't matter if you are dealing with busy, responsive or unresponsive people... if you don't get a response, you will follow up again and again until you are acknowledged.

- **Non-negotiable:** Recognize that the job of someone who deals with any other person is to follow-up with them and make sure they do what they say they will do.

- **Balloons in the air:** I picture following up like keeping balloons in the air. If there are twenty key things going on around me, I make sure I touch them all at least once per day to keep them in the air and move the process forward. Even if all it does is remind your employees and contractors that you are paying attention and you haven't forgotten about X project, it's worth it. It keeps me on my toes, too.

- **Turn a sample into an event:** When we send out a press sample, we receive an email from UPS when it's delivered... and I follow up with the reporter right then and there to see how they like it. Sometimes, we'll even get on a video chat and I'll talk them through the features in a live demo. How powerful, memorable and unique do you think that experience is? It turns receiving another product sample in a box into a one-on-one opportunity to demonstrate not only my product, but my passion.

- **Follow ups extend to customers, too:** Email marketing is critical for this process, and every opportunity you have to connect with a customer is an opportunity to bring them deeper into your world. We use automated emails to ask customers to leave a review about their product a couple weeks after purchase, and check in with them from time to time. If a customer speaks to a customer service agent and tells them they are buying our product for a trip, we'll follow up with them with a personal note when they are back to ask how it was. Laura started doing this years ago, and it's brilliant.

- **Retargeting:** We even use an advertising technique called retargeting to serve online ads specifically to people who have visited our site but not purchased anything (yet). We were one of the earliest companies using retargeting, and I still love it when people tell me that they've been seeing my ads everywhere recently and didn't realize we were so big! I guess even though it's been around for awhile, many people haven't picked up on how it's done. It's a powerful, automated way to follow up.

I could write a whole book on following up, and maybe I will. But for now, know that every single success I've had in business can in some way be attributed to following up.

The Scott OS: Measure Back

Measuring back goes hand-in-hand with following up. While following up goes from you to someone else, measuring back is essentially you following up with yourself.

(Ideally) if I spend a dollar, I track the effect of having spent that dollar. With a primarily online business, this is incredibly easy. I'm a fan of Google Analytics, and we have used it to track our online traffic and sales, and our online ad spending and results, for close to a decade at the time I'm writing this.

Perhaps you've noticed that I'm goal-oriented. Well, if you don't measure back, you don't know if you succeeded or failed. If you don't set a goal, you don't know if you made it, or how close you got.

There have been a few times where we clearly failed to measure back and it cost us money. Once, we made some adjustments to our shipping rates and didn't discover we were losing money from that for several months. Re-read that sentence: I used the word "once" very deliberately.

The only good mistakes are those not repeated.

I think a lot of people fail to measure back because they don't want to be called to the carpet or to hold their shortcomings up to the light (even if it's just them seeing it). Passion drives me. Fear drives me. Competitiveness drives me... I even use a wearable fitness tracker just to see how many steps I take every day. Measuring back is what I do to engage all those emotions within the context of hard numbers.

If there's a downside to how I measure back, it's that I don't congratulate myself enough when we win. But win or lose, you don't know if you don't measure back.

I'm always willing to try new things and take risks, but the only times I feel like something has failed - truly failed - is when we didn't measure back immediately and course correct based on the hard reality of the numbers.

The Scott OS: Use Technology

Apple. Google. Microsoft.

Massive companies who develop products that entertain and inform, but ultimately provide tools for personal productivity. With the billions of dollars that flow through them and every tech-based, VC-funded startup in Silicon Valley and New York, why on earth would I NOT use every technological advantage I can find?

If I can find technical tricks and tools that allow me to double my productivity every day, I can go twice as far in half the time. Wait... don't do the math on that, but know that I can get a lot more done and squeeze every second of active time for all it's worth.

- **Follow ups:** When I send an email and I need to follow up about it 3 days later, I don't write it on a Post-It note... there are apps for that. I like Mailbox and Sanebox, and they're 100x better than doing everything with a calendar.

- **Email, not calls:** I may be able to talk faster than I type, but if I tried to replace all my email conversations with talking, I could probably get 1/10th of my workload done each day. Last month's stats on my inbox showed I sent 9,000 emails and received 27,000 email threads. That breaks down to about 300 emails per day. Email is my tool of choice for moving the action forward.

- **Videos:** In 2008 I flew to Chicago, hired a video crew, rented a cavernous green screen studio and shot a video about my flagship product, the Travel Vest.* Today, I have a GoPro and shoot videos on the greenscreen on the first floor of our office. Technology can't always make up for the creativity of a great shooter and editor, but it certainly gets you into the game faster.

---

* Watch the video here: www.scottevest.com/vestvideo

- **Recording inspiration:** Technology allows your mind to work as fast as possible, and then act on great ideas at an appropriate time. IBM's Thomas Watson made every employee carry a notepad called a ThinkPad to write down inspirations and ideas as they popped up. The tools are better now, but the concept is the same. Don't trust that you'll remember something later. Document it NOW. Depending on where I am, I sometimes send audio files to employees, but Siri also works well for shorter messages.

- **Automatic reminders:** People don't fully understand and leverage the deeper capabilities of the devices they are already carrying. For example, you can tell your iPhone "when I leave here, remind me to take my keys" and it will remind you when your location changes. It's insanely easy to set up reminders on your phone, and most people never use that functionality.

- **Collaboration:** A Word doc? A Word doc? Why would you send me a Word doc if we need to collaborate on something? I get your file, open it and make some changes. Just as I'm about to email it back to you, you email me that I should use this NEW version of it instead. What now? This is why I use Google docs for any document that requires collaboration. In fact, this book was written in Google docs.

- **Checklists:** We have a rule at SCOTTeVEST: if you need to do any process more than twice, you need to document it with a checklist. Usually, these reside as templates in Basecamp, which we use for project and task management. New product launching? No problem... follow the checklist. You can't miss a step if you follow a checklist and pay attention.

The Scott OS: Focus on making money

I'm in business to make money. Period.

I don't care if venture capitalists don't look at profitability as a key metric. I don't care if Mark Cuban says a thousand times that the only way to start a business is with OPM (Other People's Money). And I don't care if that makes me look or sound "unsophisticated" in some circles.

I have tremendous respect for Andy Dunn from Bonobos, but it doesn't make sense to me how a company founded in 2007 has yet to make a profit, and has raised $120MM. Isn't the idea that a company - let alone a startup - is too big of an idea to fail what got our country into massive, macroeconomic trouble?

My business has a solid base in business fundamentals, like making a profit, then reinvesting that profit in the company so you can make more profit.

I understand how Silicon Valley startups convince people to let them do it, but for me:

The buck stops here, in one of my many perfectly engineered SCOTTeVEST pockets.

(Hey, I'm a passionate, personal promoter… I had to get in one more mention!)

CHAPTER 6.1
Alternate Endings

Some of my favorite parts of movies like *Fast Times at Ridgemont High* are seeing all the "where are they now" montages at the end of the film. I also love blooper reels and seeing all the unused takes that didn't make it into the final film that in some cases are even better than the movie as a whole.

Creating this book was a lot like taking a trip down memory lane, from the dark and scary bad sections of the lane to the bright, sunny, Disney-fied parts of town. But through it all, one question kept popping up:

What if?

Here are a couple "what ifs" that crossed my mind. Perhaps you can relate to those times when it was heads or tails, and everything that followed in your life was based on the tumble of a single coin. Maybe it's time for you to flip one and change the course of your life today.

If you like these "what ifs" as much as I do, we included some more at the very end of the book. Some are fun, some are dumb, some are dark and some are just one decision shy of being my reality.

What if... I took a deal for SCOTTeVEST on *Shark Tank*?

"Hello?" I said into my cell phone in the back room of the *Shark Tank* set. I got through to Woz, and he had some sage advice for me: make a deal.

I walked back into the *Shark Tank* knowing what I had to do. I was going to make a deal - one that included TEC and SCOTTeVEST - but I wasn't just going to take the first deal offered. I was going back in to negotiate.

They only showed about two minutes of it on the screen, but in reality the offers and counter-offers flew for 20 minutes. Kevin and Robert were making some headway, or in other words, they were starting to see things from my perspective.

The deal on the table evolved from them joining forces for $1,000,000 and 30% of my company to $1.5 million for 20%. Another catch: since they considered the retail part of the business to be the valuable chunk, we were now talking about SCOTTeVEST only. TEC would not be part of the deal anymore.

The cat was out of the bag, and I said "SCOTTeVEST" at least 30 times. The word made it on air six times, and traffic - and sales - went through the roof.

But just as we were about to close the deal, there was a *Shark Tank* turn-around. Mark Cuban opened his mouth and said that he wanted to be part of the deal. He said he'd back me, but I had to decide in 30 seconds, "tick tock tick tock." Of course, the deal came with stipulations. Since I was so good at defending patents, I had to be willing to protect all of Mark's, too. He wanted to keep me under this thumb.

I was about to participate in a fourway with Mark Cuban.

We all shook hands on it, and unlike a surprising number of *Shark Tank* deals that fall apart in the details after the cameras stop rolling, we actually went into business. Kevin and Robert contributed contacts and cash, but Mark was a very active partner.

He still gave me shit about my "bullshit patent" but I always reminded him about how much that bullshit patent was part of the magic behind SCOTTeVEST making money for all of us. The courtside seats were a nice perk, but the private jet picking me up for the game was even better. Flying in to Sun Valley to drop me off one day, Cuban realized something: this was a really beautiful place.

He had been making more money than ever before - partially thanks to the global clothing brand we had been building as a team - but life was burning him out. There was something fun and serene about the mountains around Sun Valley. Something that reminded him of happier days.

It struck him that he needed to live here, and he quickly bought a home. Of course, like any mountain town that has active seasons and quiet seasons, he needed something to keep him occupied and socially engaged year round, so he went back to his roots and opened a disco. Reaching back into his distant past, he once again picked up the mantle of disco dance instructor.

He seemed to be having fun again, but the tabloids weren't kind. He became distracted by what I could only call Saturday night fever, and began neglecting his everyday duties. I have no idea how he could have fallen so far, so fast, but he even reached the point where he asked me for a loan. I think it was for a laser lighted disco ball for the club (which had lost money hand over fist and foot over feet since day one).

I offered to buy out his shares of SCOTTeVEST at a healthy discount. It was the least I could do to help him keep some shred of whatever dignity he had left. After some hemming and hawing, I eventually staged a hostile takeover of all his properties.

In other words... I won.

What if... I took Laura up on her offer to support me while I became a yoga instructor?

"Hello?" I said into my desk phone when it rang with the gentle sound of a meditation gong. I hadn't touched a cell phone in a year.

"I'm very sorry, but all of our classes and seminars are filled up. Might I suggest you look into one of our DVD programs?"

I rarely answered the phone any more, but when I did, it was usually someone trying desperately to get into one of my yoga classes or seminars. Following the dozens of articles about me - the lawyer who gave up the law to become a yoga instructor - I was already spread too thin.

I had become a guru of sorts for lawyers who hated their jobs and were seeking inner peace. They said the DVDs helped, but there's nothing like learning yoga in person. It had only been a couple years since Laura offered to support me while I became a yoga instructor if that was what I felt my calling to be. A few months of training and certification later, and I was officially there, but what really set me apart was my story.

I told that story about being miserable and finding peace at least a thousand times. It had been my inspiration and passion, but lately it was starting to wear on me. Nearly all of my students were lawyers. I told them that all of the meditation and yoga in the world won't save them if they keep going back into the belly of the beast.

The pressure of being the sole source of inspiration and passion started to grind down on me, and my studios started to look like the law offices I hated. Despite the money - which was great - I knew I had to do something else. I had to follow a higher calling.

It wasn't enough for me to just be a messiah for lawyers leading them into a better life with a more flexible back and stylish (Scott Jordan branded, of course) yoga mats under their arms. I had come to a hard decision, but a necessary one:

Yoga was an interesting departure from the law, but I had to pursue my destiny.

It was time for me to change careers and become a champion breeder of poodles.

About two weeks into my new career, I realized it's all done by hand, so now I own a McDonald's franchise, my favorite restaurant. Currently, I am the only McDonald's franchise holding out and still selling supersized fries.

Would you like fries with that? (It's still better than practicing law.)

What if... writing this book got me on *Colbert, Kimmel, Fallon and the Daily Show with Jon Stewart*?

To quote Gene Wilder as Willy Wonka from the original *Charlie and the Chocolate Factory*:

"...don't forget what happened to the man who suddenly got everything he ever wanted. He lived happily ever after."

EPILOGUE
Measuring Back

The journey from starting this book to finishing it was actually pretty short. Having a few false starts during the initial phases cut into our time, but it was essentially written in just four weeks. Of course, writing it was just the beginning. Many hours were spent editing, fact-checking, creating graphics and formatting it for the various outlets through which it is available.

Writing is not an end unto itself. Regardless of how quickly I put words on the page, the ultimate goal was to have people read the book, and more importantly, to like it. Originally, I only viewed writing the book as a means to an end, but in the course of creating it, it has become so much more than that. The process reminded me of the first things I did to become successful, and how measuring back to them from time to time is how I can stay successful. Everyone reading this has that same need to measure back, and I suggest you exercise it often.

There is a common thread I've discovered among all the most successful people I've met: passion. Having it is not enough… you need to express it, own it, share it and embrace it. I was fortunate enough to learn this lesson early, and it's been a driving force for SCOTTeVEST. Sometimes, that's all you have to keep you going… and sometimes that's all you need!

Being a passionate promoter is based on – drumroll please – having an abundance of passion. Owning a business does *not* require passion. Owning a wildly successful business that people want to connect with on a deep level does. Knowing which variety of entrepreneur you want to be is a good start toward fulfilling your potential in life, love and business.

So, in my final words to you (unless you decide to read the "Deleted Scenes" next) I hope you were entertained by this book, by my ups and downs. Well, I hope you didn't enjoy my downs too much.

I'm still pushing the envelope. I'm still working fast and moving fast, but my goal is for SCOTTeVEST to become as much of a well-oiled machine as possible. In the same way that I've found my ideal role, I want to help my employees find their own clarity and personal freedom. And I want to see how much more personal freedom I can experience, too.

Fairly recently, I forgave my father. I don't hate him anymore. I know that regardless of the method, he was ultimately the force that pushed me to succeed. I did attempt to reconcile with him when I moved to Sun Valley, but it fell on deaf ears. Three short months later, when I was standing outside the press room at the Consumer Electronics Show, my sister called me to tell me he died.

I was on the cusp of my dream, and he never saw me achieve it. I discovered that I was indeed mentioned in his will... just not in any way I would want to be mentioned. The document stated, "for the purposes of this Will, my Children shall exclude Scott."

In a legal document – his final legal document – he defined his children to specifically exclude me. I was shocked and hurt in a way I had never and could never have been hurt before. It took a lot of time, but I've finally gotten over it. Getting to live the life I love is much better than harboring resentment. To me, that's winning.

If you enjoyed the book, please tell someone about it. Let's see what you learned about being a passionate promoter!

If you have any comments, or want to interview me for your top rated primetime talk show (hint hint), I'm easy to reach. Email me at scott@scottevest.com or call my cell: 208-806-1472. Clearly, I'm constantly on social media, so don't be shy about reaching out. Tell me what you think about the book. I'll do my best to get back to everyone.

Be Passionate.

Deleted Scenes

What if... Woz did the iPod spoof?

"Hello?" I said into my cell phone, not recognizing the number on the caller ID.

"Scott, it's Woz." None of my friends would have thought this would be a funny gag to play on me, so I knew it was really him.

"We just finished the shoot," he continued, "and I think the video is going to turn out great. The crew was very funny, and I had a lot of fun dancing around and filming it. In fact, I had such a great time I think I'm going to try to get on that show *Dancing with the Stars*."

"Woz - that's great!" I replied. "So happy we could work together on this."

"My pleasure, Scott. It's a shame we couldn't meet up this time. Hopefully soon. I think the spoof is going to be hilarious and I can't wait to see the final product."

My next call was to the video director/shooter/editor. I relayed to him that Woz enjoyed the experience and pushed him hard on the completion date. He reminded me of the terms of the original deal we made: he would get 10 cents for every view the video got over 1 million. In retrospect, I probably should have renegotiated after Woz offered to be in it. It was too late now.

About a week later, and with barely any changes from me (a rare occurrence), the video debuted on YouTube. When Woz said we would meet up "hopefully soon," he was right.

The video went viral thanks in large part to the strong online tech community that loved everything Apple. YouTube was "slashdotted" when the popular site covered the story of the video, and gave a behind-the-scenes look at the making of it. We topped 5 million views in a week.

Woz was invited on the talk show circuit by everyone from MSNBC to the *Today Show* to *The Colbert Report*. As another testament to his generosity, he invited me along and shared equal screen time with me. Just as the buzz began to die down, it was announced that the producers of *Dancing with the Stars* saw the iPod spoof video and invited Woz to compete because of it.

By popular demand, he did a version of the "iPod Shuffle" as his dance came to be known, and that name inspired Apple to name their new device the iPod Shuffle. The dance became an instantly recognizable part of his TV persona, and was like his signature move at the end of every dance... like a touchdown ritual. The last gesture - putting his hands into his pockets with a final flourish - linked him inextricably to SCOTTeVEST.

SCOTTeVEST sold out. Literally and completely. We sold every stitch, every pocket of inventory. I started taking pre-orders again and the pre-orders for future items totaled nearly as much as we had sold in the history of SCOTTeVEST to date.

There was a buzz in the Silicon Valley VC community that SCOTTeVEST was a hot property. Google foresaw a trend toward wearable computers, and what's more wearable than clothing? Apple saw the same trend.

I had some of the biggest choices ahead of me: acquisition, IPO or both?

We went IPO and I retained 51% with Apple and Google splitting most of the rest. We rang the bell together at the NASDAQ.

What if... I never got that call from Hammacher on my darkest day in the shrink's office?

"Hello?" I said into my cell phone, the air heavy with anticipation.

Mark Oster, my hypnotherapist, sat across from me in his chair while I leaned forward on the couch. I was expecting a call back from Hammacher Schlemmer about whether they wanted my vests for their catalog or not. This was a make-or-break day, and a make-or-break moment. If it was a yes, I was in business. All my mental ills would vanish in a moment and Mark would lose me as a patient. Still, I think he was rooting for me.

If it was a no, then I was fucked. No job, broken dream, a failure. My father would be right. My former lawyer co-workers would be right. Even worse, I would have no idea what to do next.

"Hello?!" I repeated with more intensity, more anxiety, more urgency.

"Oh, hey Scott, this is Joe from Hammacher Schlemmer. I'm really sorry, but we're not going to be able to carry your vests. We're just not really getting the concept and..."

It felt like I was hit in the head with a brick. I hung up the call.

"I'm sorry, Scott. Truly I am." Mark's voice was genuine and soothing, but I was stuck in the tornado of thoughts tearing up my mind. "Scott. SCOTT!"

I startled back into awareness of my surroundings. What felt like a steel box with walls collapsing even smaller around me became his office once again.

"Yes, doctor?" I asked, unsure whether he actually was a doctor or not.

"We still have thirty minutes left. Let's continue."

There could be no continuing for me. No next steps, no... nothing. This wasn't a slow, creeping fear that seeps into your soul. This was the fear of a pack of angry wolves appearing behind you. A fear that says fight AND flight... whatever works as long as it gets you out of here.

"Scott, you look like a potted plant."

Involuntarily, my head pulled back. "What?"

"Scott, you look like a potted plant."

I had no idea what he meant by that, and I told him so.

"Scott, you were spinning. We need to interrupt that pattern so you can start thinking in an orderly fashion. Take a deep breath, hold it for four seconds and then exhale. And again. Now again. Close your eyes and imagine yourself as a potted plant. Don't - Scott, stop - don't try to rationalize it, just go with it. Scott - BREATHE.... Good. Now, imagine what you look like as a potted plant, the color of the pot, the material and texture, the shape and color of each leaf...."

As he continued to talk in his professionally-prescribed monotone voice, I did feel things starting to fall into place. Of course, each time he said "potted" or "pot" I could only think of a marijuana plant, which amused me a little. I felt myself going deeper and deeper into - something - as my body relaxed from my scalp and face muscles, through my chest and back and all the way down to my toes.

I heard his words continuing in the background, but it felt like I was floating in a warm, bath-like pool. I still felt my intensity, but I felt physically dulled. My mind remained clear.

A plan began to crystallize. I would call my contact who worked with Mickey Segal and get a job there. Of course there were rumors the Feds were looking into him, but the guy owned this town. Even if he did get in trouble, his company and holdings would continue without him.

The call was brief, as was the interview. I had never expected to actually be interviewing with the man himself. After all, I was a lawyer, and I'm sure he had plenty of lawyers. We hit it off. It turns out that he loved racing (well, horse racing) but my passion for cars struck a nerve with him. Dispensing all formalities, he hired me on the spot.

I don't know what I was so afraid of. Being a lawyer in his organization was nothing like being a lawyer at the firms where I had been working. There were dinners, meetings with business owners and politicians, and there was no tracking of billable time. I wouldn't have come close to 200 hours per month even if anyone was keeping score. And for that, the pay was undoubtedly great. I even got to accompany him in a helicopter across town to make a meeting when the traffic was gridlocked thousands of feet below.

Laura was happy because I was happy, but there was always some doubt behind her eyes. She knew I wasn't doing anything illegal, but something smelled funny.

Eventually, an indictment did come down. The Feds raided the office, seized box after box after box of files, and carted my boss off in handcuffs. I coordinated efforts with his high-priced and favor-indebted legal team to make sure he had everything he needed. Three weeks had passed when I heard a knock on my office door, and saw the lead defense lawyer standing there. He pointed to me then curled his finger a few times to motion me over.

"Yeah Aaron, what do you nee---" I said until I was cut off mid-sentence by two FBI agents pushing me face first into the wall. The ratcheting sound of the cuffs around my wrists gave me all the answer I needed.

Sitting in jail, I worked through all the ways I could have been set up to be the fall guy. A few pieces here and there maybe, but this was ridiculous. It wasn't until the charges were announced that I understood the full extent of it, and after seven years in federal prison I still hadn't quite figured out every piece of the deception, the betrayal.

I felt like a wrongly accused lawyer stuck in the middle of a real life Scott Turow novel.

Laura stood by me through the trial, but the fact that I was stupid enough to be duped like that eroded her respect for me. She has no tolerance for stupid. I had no will to fight for her or anything from prison, and she left me. I don't blame her.

When I got out, I had a sick laugh at the fact that I could NEVER be a lawyer again. At least that part of my wish came true. Oh, and I got a tattoo!

"When I snap my fingers you will cease being a potted plant, open your eyes and wake up. Three, two, one," - snap!

I awoke with a start and frantically touched my chest, arms and face. The crude India Ink and safety-pin prison tattoo of a Porch 911 [sic] was no longer covering the back of my hand. I was alive, I was awake, I was not a felon and I was still in my hypnotherapist's office.

"So Scott, do you know now what you need to do?" he asked as calmly as can be.

"Absolutely," I replied.

That day, I went out, bought some gardening supplies, ceramic planters and grow lights. It took years of hard work, but today I am the largest grower of "medicinal" marijuana in the entire Midwest. I'm now vying for the title of Czar of legal pot as legalization spreads across the country.

Pioneer Cabin, Sun Valley, ID – 9 mile hike. Known to be one of Ernest Hemingway (and Scott and Laura's) favorite haunts.
Hemingway may have been there first.

And I've never gone under hypnosis or worked as a lawyer ever again.

What if... I took over my family business?

"Hello?" I said into my cell phone.

226

"Scott, it's your father. I need to tell you something."

He proceeded to tell me a story that I never thought I would hear from him. He told me there was an offer on the table to buy the family business. A good offer. An offer that could send him into a comfortable retirement. And he told me he was turning it down.

"Scott, I need you to promise me. To really, really promise me that you won't make me regret not selling the business. You need to step it up. Can you do that?"

I nodded, then realizing he couldn't see me over the phone, I said, "Yes."

I was in the family business, and within five years I WAS the family business. My mother passed away, but my father and I drew closer together. Honestly, it was nothing emotional… it was only that I made him money.

After he showed a little faith in me by deciding to keep the business in the family, something opened up. I started to take my work seriously. I saw the effect that I could have on people in their time of need - and before - and I approached cemetery sales with some compassion. It actually became something I felt passionate about.

This translated into money. Good money. My father was happy since he could retire, and he knew that I wouldn't destroy the business he built up over so many years. We finally had something in common, and it turned out to be… money.

From this point, things could have played out in a few different ways:

My father and I might have a good relationship based on the business. I would still be living in Cincinnati, enjoying the Country Club life, married to a nice Jewish girl who couldn't cook to save her soul but was a loving mother to our kids. I'd splurge on a sports car to compensate for my growing waistline, and been in the hospital with my dad when he died. All in all, it would be a fairly happy but uninteresting life, and you never would have crossed paths with me.

Another scenario is that the family business is split between my two sisters and me after my father dies. I continue to run it, but they each get a third of what I make without spending a minute working, just because their names were on the will. We fight over money constantly, and my brothers-in-law expect a raise every six months even when they don't show up for work three days in a row. My life is messy, and each of my expenses on the company ledger is subject to my sisters' scrutiny. I keep writing checks to them each month based on my work for no good reason, and life sucks.

My third fantasy is that I apply the same spark that makes SCOTTeVEST successful and make a splash in the world of cemetery sales. The family business is highly lucrative - much better than my father was able to make it - and I realize I have a knack for it. I start buying up every cemetery in the country and become known as the Donald Trump of Cemeteries. My competitors call me the "Donald Trump of the Dead." People are dying to get into my properties. Laura and I happen to meet, and life goes on rather happily with our poodle family.

Eventually, I branch out into real estate for the living, too. Tired of being nicknamed "the Donald Trump of Cemeteries" I bought his company and renamed it SCOTTESTATE. We open a themed amusement park called SCOTTeLAND next month.

What if... my recurring nightmare came true?

"Hello?" I said into my cell phone.

"Hello? HELL-O?!" I repeated, louder and more intensely as it continued to ring loudly and incessantly, regardless of how many times I tried to answer it.

After a minute of screaming at the mocking, ringing phone, consciousness seeped in and I realized it was a dream. The phone that wouldn't stop ringing was really my alarm clock.

I had been having the nightmare again. But the nightmare I awoke to was even worse than the one I dreamt... because it was an inescapable reality from which I would not awaken.

I was in my third dead end job with my fourth asshole boss. After I couldn't get my idea for a fishing vest with pockets for gadgets to take off - and yeah, even I admit now it was a stupid idea - I had to find a job. I tried life in a law firm as "Of Counsel," but every day was like being the fat kid when it was time to pick teams for baseball. I didn't want to put up with the bullshit anymore, so I decided the corporate world was a better choice.

But it was really the same choice. Since I was a lawyer, they attached me to any project that was even tangentially related to the law, then they'd yell at me when I didn't know the obscure answer to something lawyerly.

"But you're a lawyer, aren't you???"

I still couldn't shake the scarlet L. My work was devoid of passion. My life was devoid of passion. My nightmares and my waking life are the same.

I got fat and moved to the burbs. I became the person I feared I could become: the mediocre, lawyerly version of myself.

This is an actual nightmare I have every few months, and it feels like a fate worse than death.

What if... I ran for office?

"Hello?" I said into my cell phone, nervous because it came from my campaign manager's office.

This was not my first election campaign, and with every election campaign, you either win or lose. I had never lost yet. This would be the biggest disappointment if it was a disappointment, but it would be my clearest stepping stone to the White House if it was a victory.

I've always been fascinated by politics. I would describe myself as a Reagan Democrat or an Obama Republican. I'm definitely a contradiction in terms, but that was what people found appealing about me. The same-old same-old of politics wore down on people, and while I might not have been a breath of **fresh** air, at least I was something different.

I was a terrible politician, and people liked that.

I'm too transparent to lie. I can't promise things to people if I have no intention of keeping them. In a political landscape built around "hope" where the tomorrows never lived up to the promises, my jaded, almost cynical view of politics resonated with voters.

It started locally in Sun Valley. One day while I was out walking the poodles, I slipped on some ice on the street and broke my elbow (again, same side as before I went on *Shark Tank*). There was four inches of ice built up on the road. No one in town knows how to plow properly, and apparently using salt could somehow harm trout in a stream two miles away.

I thought the whole thing was bullshit. For a mountain town whose income is based on winter tourists, having dangerous conditions was unacceptable. My arm in a sling, I appeared before the town council.

The next year, I joined the town council, then soon thereafter I led the town council. When yet another airport-bathroom-sex-scandal hit Idaho (Google "Larry Craig Idaho"), I was able to run as the first Independent in Idaho. If I won this election for the open Senate seat, I could follow Obama's path from first term Senator to President.

In my run for the Senate, I picked up an unlikely political advisor: Sarah Palin. It turns out that she had been to a survivalist/prepper convention in Alaska and bought a SCOTTeVEST. She wanted to always be ready to run for office, run after a moose AND to run for her life, and the dozens of pockets in my vests helped her do exactly that. Strangely, at first she was confused... she was the only person ever to confuse my company for SCOTT USA. Hmmmm.

My campaign was not too outlandish to her. She had been the mayor of a town smaller than mine, then became the governor of a state with fewer people than Idaho, and then made a bid for VP. She could relate to my trajectory.

My second "in" with her was that she was great friends with the Governor of Idaho, Butch Otter. (I shit you not... Google "Butch Otter Idaho.")

"Hello?" I repeated into my phone. I won.

So... who thinks I should actually run for office?

What if... I became an author and went on a national speaking tour?

Hmmm... I just became an author. How did I do? Obviously, I crave validation. Do you think I should go on a national speaking tour? Let me know at www.SCOTTeVEST.com/book

THE END

See Scott as 00? at www.scottevest.com/quantum

SCOTT JORDAN WILL RETURN IN...

His next thrilling book about how any entrepreneur can live their dreams:

"From Paradise, With Love"

About the Photographer

Photo by Thomas Hawk

"What makes a great portrait is oftentimes the emotion shared by a subject with a photographer. I've had the privilege of photographing Scott Jordan many times and am honored that he chose some of these portraits for the front and back covers of this book. Like a great photograph, what makes a great book is similarly the emotion shared by the writer with the reader, here Scott delivers an equally compelling version of his story to the world." – **Thomas Hawk**, ThomasHawk.com

About the co-Author

Thom O'Leary:

- Makes letters into words and words into sentences
- Makes lines into designs and designs into products
- Sees the view from space and through the microscope
- Makes it happen and gets it done

Find him at:
www.FixerGroup.com/books

OK, THIS IS REALLY THE END. CLOSE THE BOOK NOW.

(And get 20% off anything at SCOTTeVEST with the promo
code found at www.scottevest.com/bookend)

I'm outta here!

Made in the USA
Lexington, KY
13 November 2014